STRIKING A MATCH IN A STORM

Andrew McNeillie was born in North Wales and read English at Magdalen College, Oxford before becoming an editor and publisher. For a key period in his life, he was literature editor at Oxford University Press. He has also held a chair in English at Exeter University where he is now Emeritus Professor. He is the founding editor of the magazine *Archipelago* and runs the Clutag Press. His memoir *Once* appeared in 2009 from Seren. His Carcanet poetry collections are *Nevermore* (2000), *Now, Then* (2002), *Slower* (2006), *In Mortal Memory* (2010) and *Winter Moorings* (2014). His memoir, *An Aran Keening*, was published in 2001.

Striking a Match in a Storm

New & Collected Poems

ANDREW McNEILLIE

CARCANET POETRY

First published in Great Britain in 2022 by
Carcanet
Alliance House, 30 Cross Street
Manchester, M2 7AQ
www.carcanet.co.uk

A CIP catalogue record for this book is
available from the British Library.

ISBN 978 1 80017 233 3

Book design by Andrew Latimer
Printed in Great Britain by SRP Ltd, Exeter, Devon

The publisher acknowledges financial
assistance from Arts Council England.

for Diana

Knowing I have never erred in anything
but in the things that have mattered to me most.
Luis Rosales

Late sang the blackie but it stopt at last.
The river still ga'ed singin' past.
Hugh MacDiarmid

CONTENTS

from *Nevermore* (2000)

from *Now, Then* (2002)

from *Slower* (2006)

from *In Mortal Memory* (2010)

–Song in Winter–

–At Sea–

from *Losers Keepers* (2011)

Milton's Italian Sonnets translated for *The Complete
Works of John Milton* Vol. III (OUP, 2012)

from *Winter Moorings* (2014)

from Making Ends Meet (2017)

Meanwhile (New Poems)

from NEVERMORE (2000)

PLATO'S AVIARY

'Miss Kershaw would identify the bird as the bar-tailed godwit or
"yarwhelp"… the godwit being called "yarwhelp" because it resembles
the curlew.'
Ida Gordon, footnote to *The Seafarer*

(i) NEVERMORE

The ravens we knew cast no shadow then,
Honking and cronking over the bryn
Head-over-heels in courtship's light
-hearted flight at first of spring.

Wheeling so high, they went out into orbit
Somewhere beyond the cwm,
A shadow falling only after
All these years, like light from stars.

(ii) GREY-LAGS (*Anser anser*)

They so rarely reach here now
You'd be forgiven for thinking you're dreaming,
The dream of eternity, or some such,
You with your goose-wing westward prospect,
And a puddle blowing at your door:

Demisting your spectacles in a cloud of linen,
Squinting across the flapping morning
To see how their true aim's flown,

With an arrow-head as variable as any head,
Wavering in a smudged heaven.

(iii) WHEATEAR (*Oenanthe oenanthe*)

As if those walkers could be troubled
Distracted from their confidences
To leave the path and cast in circles
After your decoying loops and glances
From stone to stone among
The bleached and thinning grasses
To find your clutch
Cupped at the heart of silence here.

As if even one of them could name you
Or know you by your stony chatter
But you rehearse regardless
To be on the safe side
Of this shadowed mountain till
Kingdom come as once below
Time was the people sang
Their hearts out everlasting.

(iv) CORNCRAKE (or Landrail *Crex crex*)

Spring slips him in through a gap
In a stone wall, a secret agent

Bargaining with the underworld
Against sleep, a bomb

With a slow time-fuse, an old man
Winding all our clocks on, and back.

(v) CURLEW (*Numenius arquata*)

So burdened with sorrow that
Its beak is bowed down by it:
A Campbell mouth, *whaup* in my lost lexicon.
But of leaden skies on the moor
The virtuoso elegist, even in spring:
Always the one I want to hear again.

Last night I dreamt I woke
With one beside me, its head upon the pillow,
Eye serenely closed, and, however dark its dream,
I saw at once that it was really smiling,
Not grieving, but upside down,
So as not to give the game away.

(vi) TERNS (Common and Arctic, *Sterna hirundo* and *macrura*)

Rule of three? Escapees from Matisse,
Playing scissors-paper-stone along the beach.
Who'd second-guess you but by luck?
Not this raised strand of storm-stressed shingle
Petered to sand where your pebble eggs lie nestled.
Not summer's page of vanishing blue
So slow to unfold its origami of stars.
And not these thole-pinned oars that snip a wake of puddle
Litter where you mob and scold, and dive
For fry, and I spin my line to the bay.
Maybe only the quicksilver dune that's never still,
Shimmering grain on grain, can match
Your lightning wing-blades? So odd
You seem to have chosen me to halo,
Who haven't an earthly, with my two wooden oars,

Not even now you're flown, wherever it is
You fly to, and I have all the time in the world.

(vii) LAPWING (or Peewit *Vanellus vanellus*)

You cannot will them back, but why,
when I can recall at will
their lapping sorcery,
to the precise peet or peewit
of their billowed flight,
should this empty morning's grey
bowl of sky above the farmland
remind me first of the one
that landed in our hearth
on Christmas day, uncrestfallen,
soot green-black and white
with metal legs and feet
and wings you might
operate by pulling on a wire?
a decoy from the continent, a gift,
an ornament, a childish toy to us,
that had us charmed,
if never for a moment fooled -
when I'd much sooner think of them
in their magician's night-and-day-
under-over-plover-cover-lapping light,
and sing them, as we then could,
tumbling over the winter wheat,
making the air throb, their wings
in mittens for the cold, their crazy wits
rivals to the mad March hare,
as now to me, in sorrow,
shadow boxing here.

(viii) ADERYN DU (Blackbird *Turdus merula*)

i.m. Hughie Bach

No more a soul of fixed abode:
Missing, though seen upon the road –
The low road high in blowing weather,
The low road to the racing river –
Ardent for nothing but his loss.

Bare branches and wild sky god bless:
Tenebrous blackbird on the gusting air,
Where October's river, hole-in-corner,
Digs deep to drown the depths of winter,
And sings its own intoxicating song.

His warning spills out hurriedly, as if
He has withdrawal jitters from the demon drink.
Alarmed again, he scolds away
To skulk through shadow on shadow
Along the memory of spring.

(ix) ANOTHER TAKE ON THE BLACKBIRD

In the rocky rowan the blackbird sings
Tunes from his golden treasury
His pall-grave book of poems,
Turning phrases this way and that
In the thin leaves and evening air,
Miraculously, his eye transfixed.
His song an obolus for the ferryman.

(x) GODWIT (*Limosa limosa* or *lapponica*)

Waders splinter light, in sudden galaxies,
And surf echoes hooves, along the metalled road,
Fainter and louder, starlight in each breaker,
And the heavy dune dashes its grasses,
Its crests of marram, breaking into
A wall of light, in a heaven harbouring
Wonder at the anchored moment,
On a morning charged with spring.

Where everything seems surging to become,
I tug from the jetsam this earthbound one,
Salt-dried stiff and weightless but
Unmistakable, god knows: a godwit,
Witless, but whether a black- or a bar-tailed,
It's already flown too far away to tell.

(xi) WREN (*Troglodytes troglodytes*)

What poetry? Wired up out of light and dark,
At the mercy of seasons, genie or Houdini,
No respecter of persons: a wing and a prayer,
Seat of your pants kind of affair? Uncrowned king
Of obscurity, your music as pungent as ivy?
No fear at those great shades whose project is
To float off cathedrals and symphonies
Over the abyss and limbo there for eternity,
Consoling, constellation beyond constellation of loss,
In your little local speech of stars
And saplings and crepuscular melancholy,
A line of solder silver between sky and holly?
A tin-pot holding operation, a quick fix?
My little winter communard, sleeping how many to a bed?

(xii) CORMORANT (*Phalacrocorax carbo*)

I remember the day the old man shot one
high over the house and how it folded,
like a winded umbrella, and came down
in a thorn bush, stone dead, neck collapsed,
wings hooked up to dry for the last time.
But why still, that nervous, apprehensive wonder,
the word *skart* on my tongue for pleasure?
Why couldn't I settle to sleep that night
for thinking about it? I wasn't upset.
I didn't weep. It got what was coming to it.
It was the devil, the thief on the cross, of fish
that we might catch. Way out of range it swerved,
but the old man was a dead-eyed dick.
I'd seen him perform such miracles before.
And even if I smiled, when he laid it out
for my education in the life and death
of birds, and distinguished it from the *SHAG*,
I kept my school-yard smirk to myself, so he had
no cause to curse me for a tom fool.
Perhaps it was just those three dabs,
the size of half-a-crown, that came
flipping from its gullet alive, alive O
O, O as moist as eyes? ... Maybe.

(xiii) LITTLE STINT (*Calidris minuta*)

Stint your step to spring, unstinting,
Quick to cloud and lose yourselves
In shell-bursts, to find yourselves,
A stunt of stints, treble-voiced,
Suddenly reunited, for a stint ashore
At the storm's edge and limpid

Aftermath of the streaming strand,
The fine grains timing you
At your ankles, piping cold,
Time's stinted passage in the harsh tide.
So I come here to shiver with you
And chatter in the dying day
Of loss untold, taken at the flood.

(xiv) CHOUGH (*Coracia pyrrhocorax*)

Considering their distribution in old haunts
Of armadas where even the people
Can still bear an Iberian look, I'd like to believe
These crazy *kiaow-k'chuf* kazooers embody souls
Of red-lipped girls descended from flamenco dancers,
Or Catalonian cross-dressers in black skirts and
Red stockings, fled from the Inquisition,
Castanets clacking, castaway to flirt on cliffs
And strut their stuff above the wrecked Atlantic.

Though the authorities say the truth is other and
A while after all roads led to Caesar's Rome,
Or Ovid's exile, the soul of King Arthur
Migrated into one, which would as well explain
Why choughs are so fay and flighty, being
Deranged and *déraciné* just like me, with
My binocular visions, captive to a dream
I have lost and gained in being here before them
This day beside myself with pleasure?

(xv) WOODCOCK (*Scolopax rusticola*)

Blued gunmetal dusk conducts cold lightning
To my memory. In my blue hand then

The barrel of an Xmas pen, in a snap below freezing,
Brings you to that coast and me to myself again,
At eighteen, bedroomed to the creaking wood.
Shall I dream there for you, with guilt in my heart,
Cleaved as lightning to gunmetal? Like lightning
Your anticipated flight from the dead leaves,
Leafmeal and leavings, traceries of snow:
Little maps to get blear-eyed in, staring and
Staring crepuscule, stalking moccasin to look into
Your big black eyes too luminous my love to
Hide you, the flaw in your camouflage and
Sober bearing. Shall I fail to find you or in a
Snapshot catch you as you jink out through
The empty saplings into star-dust, blown
To the ends of the earth? Or turn instead and
Meet you *roding* by, growling like a toad,
Then tutting *tsiwick tsiwick,* at just an arm's length
In purring flight between the yew and hazel,
Your long bill pointing as if pensive at the ground:
So that even with only half my wits about me
I might reach out and catch you in my hand?

(xvi) MISTLE-THRUSH (or Stormcock *Turdus viscivorus)*

Here is the field of grass in shadow
With its bare hedge and gloomy oak.
None receives the sky but stands off
In winter mirk that will soon turn
Dark. The world's shut down like
A risky Chernobyl in whose full glare
We might all die but for this precaution,
Though die we do of seasonal boredom.

Here I recall my youth's captivity:
Just in this spot and at this hour
Out to escape the inescapable,
Mooching in fields and woods,
Half-watching a shadow-world fail
When at the corner of his Northern eye
Wings the herald, fast, with snow
And storm in stars upon its breast.

Life will change, but whether
For better or worse, take heart,
Such sudden flights and bitter-
sweet termini beneath mistle-
toe or holly wreath, are bonuses
Forever, second-looked, named twice,
Once seen never to be forgotten:
Mistle-thrush or Stormcock.

(xvii) JACKDAW (*Corvus monedula*)

   for John and Sheila McNeillie

O local shades, so much more like us than
The others, in your community and accent,
Loyalties and squabbles: good neighbours,
Chapel folk, field-workers, quarriers
And gossips, cackling all day *ky-ky* mozaic
Music to our domestic ears, routines
And little ceremonies of hearth and ash
And fallen soot, swelling to sudden
Blissful crescendi and shimmer above
The wooded bryn, now heard and
Forever through the heart's high roof.

Believe me, since we co-tenanted Coed Coch
Or that seaborne life at Tan-yr-allt,
I've travelled ways and worlds as far
As birdless Acheron and back, would strike
Your poor hearts dumb, for thirty years as I
Have been, sea-green corruptible, in love
With setting out, the better to know home
The moment I first hear you greet the day.

(xviii) YELLOWHAMMER (*Emberiza citrinella*)

The first telephone we had in our house
presided in Cyclopean silence, at the foot of the stairs.
Its big dial stared at us as we passed
as if daring us to make a call. But to whom?
It had about as much use as the front room.
But unlike that soot-scented holy of holies
it was for us ahead of its time.
For some reason its mouthpiece made me
think of the dentist, or the colossal
lower mandible of a fruit-eating tropic bird
seen in the waiting-room's *National Geographic*.
Listen deeply? I can still hear its silence,
waiting, and its shopdoor tinkle
as I lift the receiver from its cradle,
its seductive purring tone.
But ours was more like a clunky country girl,
with its plaited brown cable, on an
outpost farm, waiting for a call.
Until it came, I used to dream it might
resound with spring's hedgerow and wall-top drone
where the stave of wires hummed its backing
to a limpid lyric: the yellow-hammer's
deil, deil, deil, deil, tak ye, curse squiggled too

on its egg in the roadside nest I knew
where the holly grew in with the hazel;
or that *a little bit of bread and no*
cheese (the cheese sometimes omitted as
the authorities say; as if to show evolution in
process). But then there came other birds.
Deil, deil, deil, deil, tak ye.

(xix) TEAL (*Anas crecca*)

The proper term for this activity is roding.
Beneath the flat stare of the moon,
In from the scything estuary to glean
Or flock around fresh water,
Thick, and quick as any jump-jet wader.

Here shoots up a solitary, in exclamation.
Not saying where it came from, just
Announcing already that it's almost gone?
To disprove that one can
Ever stand for many, many a one?

As some would like to claim acclaiming
Self, and they'd be wrong,
The truth of teal and true poems being
For roder as for reader
That they know no comparison.

(xx) REDWING (*Turdus musicus*)

This Sunday walking in the park I saw you,
Frozen still, as if you meant to melt from view
Before my eyes, resisting my subpoena,
As one might cut a former lover's gaze.

But witness you must stand now none the less
To purely circumstantial evidence of loss, such as:
A youth's Cold War affair with Julie Christie,
Upon a soft and saline coast in 1960-
something, when snow as never seen since
I don't know when fell, fast and thick,
Across the heart's Siberia, a blizzard of pages torn
From a scene by Pasternak? And plodding home
The long way, for the hell of it, he met
An epic flight of heralds, overtaken by their own foreboding.
Their calls so close to *SEE! SEE! SEE! SEE!*
Made him look up to where they milled among
The flakes and fluttered in the little wood,
To perch exhausted, or fall down dazed, their eyes
Within eyes already blank, at the farthest gates.
Reds with the stare of Strelnikov, harried by the elements.
Too late, however you regard it now, to speak
Of innocence or snow. The two he succoured
With codliver drops and airing-cupboard billets
Died in their socks, should you care to know,
Redwing in the park, this February morning.

(xxi) BULLFINCH (*Pyrrhula pyrrhula*)

A true poem about you would
Make no mention of apple or bud.
You would be too fly for that.

Just the premonition of them and
You'd vanish with a blush
That somehow managed to be brazen

Leaving the ripped promise of fruit
And us perversely at the window still
Longing for you to be so bold again.

(xxii) WATER-RAIL (*Rallus acquaticus*)

As well try to walk on water
As hope to see you with my
Stalking eye and stealthy
Halted step in imitation of
Your freeze-frame motion.
But somehow in your beady
Look, the mirror-echo
Wetland of my heart
Catches a miraculous sighting.

Complicity of hunter and
Quarry they say: the one
Willing to become the other.
Up front at last and audible
Where water changes into sky
Sky clouds and turns to ink,
Foot by foot, I hold on to
Your broken railing and
Advance into the reeds.

(xxiii) GROUSE (*Lagopus scoticus*)

How did you get that lipstick on your eyebrow? So
Lavishly she kissed me in those days.

Grouse? I've no more grievance than Arenig
Head-in-cloud, dreaming of a dawning moor.

In that feral time I came of age and world now
Gone, over the hill and under it, flying in the dark,

The peat-dark of this inglorious flesh
And bog-soft dram, served me on my birthday.

DAY STAR

The outhouse lamp left on across the yard.
A farewell taken only last evening for a greeting.
Light years away it seems now, ushered out
In night-holm's evergreen aftermath.
So much hope, so little time?
Galaxies in the wings. May I share them with you?
As the Plough said to the Bear, the trick being
To suspend belief in mere appearances of things.

ELEGY

Why so many birds in the bare branches of your poems
flitting like titmice on a spring morning high in the pines?
Along your rivers and shores or plummeting down windswept skies,
tagged with Latin like shrubs, trailing banners like planes,
advertising the end of the world, or speaking Welsh? A parliament
of fowls in an age hardly rated for its inclination to govern, sing or rhyme
however inflected, or confected, of however many blackbirds,
or even warble, let alone boom, or caw, or coo, or honk, or hoot, or quack,
whoop, mimic, mewl, wail, shriek, pee-wit, or, crexing, ratchet back
the winding stars all night beneath your window,
a breath in the curtain and the moon a sea-green halo,
and the depth-charged surf full of wheeling, phosphorescent
                                        notes of waders.

In the hope you might imagine a world without them:
no thrush on the aerial; no yellow-hammer on the droning wire,
begging for a little bit of bread and no cheese, on the back-roads now
only of memory; no wren's loud voice in the winter ivy;
no chaffinch on the coldest morning ever recorded for March;
no wild swan whooping from the windswept lochan;
no ousel deafened by the stream's spring force;
no lark ascending, no redbreast whistling, no parrot either,
in Amazon or parlour. Not one. Not anywhere, ever,
heard or seen, of this or any other feather. Mourn them?
They mourn themselves, their ghosts soaring from the lost glades,
the crashing canopies, rocketing on startled wings.

THE WHITING

Snow falls when you least expect it.
A rural saying to amuse the sceptic.
But none the less
A clichéd Christmas greeting
Fooled the coast that year
With stinging flakes, as perished flocks
Of redwing refugees in comas
Fell dying through the silent branches,
Out of Scandinavia,
Or a northern elsewhere, anyway,
Its serrated horizon of pines
Sawing the blue cold of a brief day,
As glimpsed at the Odeon
By Sharif's Zhivago.

That day we went to the pier-head
And fished all evening in a yellow storm.
And as if to show
How dreams-come-true
Establish norms, the whiting rose
In blizzards from below
And stormed our hooks
At every single throw
Until they skidded round our boots
In translucent lobes of ice
Their eyes like melting snow.

EXTRAS

Never a Joseph, nor even a shepherd or wise man
but some surly angel, train-bearer,
or escort to a king, without a line to spin,
to fill a tableau or swell a curtain call,
so fitting them for life far better than
brief village stardom might. *Enter, shuffling,*
as if nudged into view by war's statistics:
History's full-backs and reserves.
Cannon fodder talent-spotted early.

LAMPREYS

for Brian Pattinson

They writhed at my feet, snake-like,
eel-like, as if hooked, and so they were,
leopard tails switching in their lust to breed,
in a dance you might call the *lampreda* or
lampetra, in the Latin vein, 'the stone-sucker',
each with its jawless mouth and rasping teeth
limpet-fast. Thirteen I saw there clearing stones
the size of bricks, pebbles, gravel,
to make their redds and lay their eggs
for the males to sperm. Then one turned to me
where I stood unpartnered and we danced.
Suckered to my wellington, she drew me deeper
down into their weaving spell, that dappled
day, the river low, and no salmon running.
And I went, my best foot forward, mesmerised,
as if they added me to my sudden knowledge of them,
in a mysterious ritual, like those dance-night girls
I knew by name but could only crave
as they shuffled to and fro, boogying together,
until one beckoned with a look for me to ask her.

IN MEMORY OF PRIVATE ROBERTS: BRITISH SOLDIER

for Eirwen, Ann and Wynn

Crossing the square in early spring,
Wreaths withered on the memorial,
Poppies bled by frost and snow,

I met Private Roberts reading
The roll call of the town's fallen.

'Armistice day? My pet aversion,'
Turning to me, his lip moist,
His thorny eye narrowed like a sniper's:
'Ior Evans? He'd never spent
A night away from home before,

Buried in Mad-a-gas-car.
Corner of a foreign field?
I doubt he'd ever heard of it.
Dei Sam? on Manchester
United's books in thirty-nine:

Buried in France. I bet
He's never remembered
At the going down of the sun
Or in the morning... Duw!
You know, I often contemplate

Siegfried Sassoon, chucking his medal away.
Never applied for mine.
All the way to Tobruk without
So much as a lance-jack's stripe,
I'm proud to say.

And Francis Ledwidge, born
The same day as Hedd Wyn,
And killed, you know, the same day
And in the same place too.
His comment: "To be called

A British soldier
While my country has
No place among nations..."'
He'd marched to Vesuvius
With Marcus Aurelius

In one breast-pocket and
The *Mabinogi* in the other,
An old campaigner
Over bog and heather
To find and fish the Serw stream:

Elusive, stubborn thread of water,
Of stygian glooms and mountain glances,
Its limpid, garrulous medium,
'Full,' as he said, 'of small trout
The length of a youth's hand.'

HAIR OF THE DOG

Rain, one-hundred per cent proof,
Intoxicates the windblown day
But doesn't keep us from our thirst,
Or make us face another way.
We plod on through the shite,
Collars up and tails down,
Addicts too of gravity and light.

On the longest binge since Noah's ark
It swells the river torrent here
Searching out old pockets for
Tumbling leaves of gold and silver,
To stand around at the road's elbow

In a froth-lipped gesture at largesse,
Digging deep, the drunken bore.

Plus ça change...... it loves to seep.
But here's enough small change
To get us dry, for a hair of the dog
To bite with light the flinty drop,
To pause with you a moist lip,
A moist eye, and raise a glass:
To the dog. To the drowned dog.

REALITIES

You do not need to be dumb
To be rendered speechless.
You do not need your theft hand severed
To find writing impossible.
You do not need an objective correlative
To spend Christmas in a murderous mood.
You do not need the literal
To compose the real.
What is it then my friend I need?
I give you in one:
Your heart's desire.

MEDITATION IN A PUBLIC GARDEN

'Ce chien est à moi, disoient ces pauvres enfants; c'est là ma place au soleil: voilà commencement et l'image de l'usurpation de toute la terre.'
Pascal, *Pensées*

Rendezvous for respite here? No way.
Melancholy the shade of gravel and the fountain
Wavering its *fleur-de-lys'* imperfect heart.
This world waits for me as if I was myself
Procured, a rare but dim shrub with a Latin
Name, dogsomething dubbed by Linnaeus, say,
And planted on a damp bench between
Leguminosae and *Cistacea*; in their case both
Damned to mourn a Mediterranean soil and sky
For life as I mourn love and youth
Unnoticed in my grief by either as I pass,
Arm-in-arm, or pause in front of me to kiss.
What flesh! To be elsewhere if I could for once
Not a guest like this at my own urn-burial,
Cheek the colour of white bread and paste,
Funeral meats, a feast of endless asphodel ahead?
There's life-pulse in the veined leaf yet,
Protest, if not enough to prompt a second look,
To make one stoop and take that tender
Sapiens sapiens label for a wonder (planted in '46!). O,
If we were creatures in a zoo, we would express
Our sadness in pacing round and round. But I
Just sit here staring at my hands, salve not slave,
Or who could bear not to look into my eyes?
Salve to my every grief and conscience?
My heart, this scant bush rocking to and fro,
Winds back upon itself like the wild rose.
But get up and go, you fool, follow your nose,

And have a gander while you can, from
Alp to Tropic, rock to hothouse rim,
And admit pleasure in this imperium?:
Over seas and under other stars than these,
For the time of year, stars that already
Prick the sky with subterranean light
From somewhere long ago, to the South,
Where pithy men I would not like, with all
Their equipage in train, lend everything
They can a name, if possible, their own,
From stick to stone, from sprig to State,
Until there is no other world to legislate.
The reason I come here, to be alone,
Unclassified, and without my maker,
To pursue a poem with pen and paper:
Against the grain, in homage to Anon.

SILENCE PLEASE & BE UPSTANDING

The day is silenced by the night,
The palace garden by a banquet,
The agents by their cover.
The dark is silenced by the moon,
The minister's mistress by her lover.
The room is silenced by a spoon
Tinkling a glass balloon.
Silence, please, and be upstanding.
Silence is an oxymoron.
Whose ghost is that upon the landing?
The state is silenced by its fear
Like princes silenced in a tower.
Cain silences Abel. Babel babel.
Light silences the star.

The spider spins in silence for the fly.
The tortoise silences the hare,
Timon Athens, Caesar Rome.
It's in the silence that it happens.
The Black Man, silenced by the White Man,
Hangs in silence from the tree.
Silence sanctions tyranny.
The sky is silenced by the sea.
A storm silences the promontory.
Silence in the wilderness is loud,
Elsewhere it stuns a crowd.
Nuremberg is silenced by a hand.
The words are silenced by the mind.
Serbia silences and... vice versa, Serbia.
The woods are silenced by the guns.
The soldiery are silenced by their wounds.
The birds are silenced by their songs.
(All's quiet on the western front.)
The lie is silenced by the lay.
Who'd silence poets may
Grant them immortality.
A poem is silenced by a commentary?
(I think not. Therefore I am.)
The church is silenced by a prayer.
Silence is the thing you vow.
Supplicants are silenced by the host,
Murderers by a Hamlet's or a Banquo's ghost.
We pass into the greater Silence.
The quick are silenced by the dead.
The dead are silenced by the quick.
The rest my friend is history, or not.
Silence fears how Denmarks rot.
Her love is silenced by pyjamas.
The ape is silenced by bananas.

Silence wall to wall surrounds us.
The truth is silenced by the family.
The lovers' toils are silenced by
Half-past-one in the morning.
It is a very silent feeling.
Staring in silence at the ceiling.
As silent at least as breathing.
So silence keeps the night awake
And in our dreams we hear it speak
How night is silenced by the day.

WISH LIST

The iceberg that makes it round the world.
The complete works of Anon.
A cape and stars above the sea.
The camel through a needle's eye.
The Life of William Shakespeare by Himself.
The first of day. Her louch look.
The sweetest fuck.
The nesting bird.
The omertá of old age.
The light at the heart of the pyramid.
The song you have by heart.
The harbour light at dawn.
The sound within the poem.
The curlew on the moor.
The wild-goose skein.
The raven rolling in a windy sky.
The world turned upside down.
Tête à tête avec Owain Glyndŵr.
Genius-in-waiting.
Winter lightning.

The last word of the old order and first of the new.
The Republic of Scotland.
The Republic of Wales.
Vision and revision.
Hindsight as foresight.
The reader read.
The people's voice.
The happy couple.
The oar's puddle.
The Tower of Babel.
The lighthouse bell.
A millpond sea.
The dune's crest in the moving air.
The tribe's oral tradition.
The other as me.
The one in B minor. The next line.
The coelacanth's mating ritual.
The girl who never returned your love.
The end of all that. The end of all this.
A new poetics. A new prosody.
The poet guilty as charged.

CORNCRAKE AS HOURGLASS

crex crex crex crex crex crex crex crex crex crex
crex crex crex crex crex crex crex crex crex
crex crex crex crex crex crex crex crex
crex crex crex crex crex crex crex
crex crex crex crex crex crex
crex crex crex crex crex
crex crex crex crex
crex crex crex
crex crex
crex
crex crex
crex crex crex
crex crex crex crex
crex crex crex crex crex
crex crex crex crex crex crex
crex crex crex crex crex crex crex
crex crex crex crex crex crex crex crex
crex crex crex crex crex crex crex crex crex
crex crex crex crex crex crex crex crex crex crex....

MORE

(i) *Odysseus at Kilmurvey*

The road taken a sea-road, harboured at heart,
Sea-green corruptible as Plato would have said.
How even now there's uplift in the thought and
Sinking, and slide and backslide, unstable dancing
In the tide's gift and weather's frown or grace.

Time alone will tell. In a snatched week's solitude,
These driftwood planks and spewed spars thrown
Down here make a start. Time alone.
To go the longest way round, via Holyhead,
Is to take the shortest way home, the man said?

My poor temperament is slight and prone
To gabble *ar lan y môr* like geese on a stubble,
A sea-stubble of threshed waves I imagine
Off Wales now. Too big for words,
The sea hasn't aged since earth began

No more its guiding lights of inert stars,
Flickering from the sunny universe above.
All resolution to be resolute mends and breaks
Like the sea and holds like it. My heart
In an embrace now of stars as sharp as whins.

Starlike too, gulls wheel and cry with light on fire
Above the crackling coast and harry heaven.
And as I go, or think of going, a sadness weighs anchor,
To find Tom Hernon dead or in his island garden?
Never go back they say, never return.

As if you could - when and to what?
Except to the drowning sea itself off Connacht-know-nothing.
I stand as he did and not as he did.
Chasten me and my sojourn baptise
Leaden sky, this side the dark strand.

Youth knows what it cannot tell and now
My telling is forgetting. To remember: I am
Already and always somewhere else, and
So are they. Time's worn us beyond recognition
Since those days? You would not believe.

Keep your threadbare name to yourself
And play the strategist for once.
Just a word told here will be a truth at least,
Sound as a pebble in the shingle. Did you ever know
A friend I had lived here? (I never did.)

(ii) *Prayer for the* Naomh Éanna

Thirty years is a lifetime in your wake and many lives
And many fares to many fairs. No voyage without a wake
And no death worthy of the name: when did you last see daybreak?
Who plies your journey now? Who tells your stories? *Naomh Éanna*
                                                    I pray for you
And all who sailed in you on those wild seas I knew.
Though just whatever comes to hand may decree what's beautiful

In time: transports of delight now make Magic of the Sea
(*Draoícht na Farraige*): *Flyer, Sprinter, Express…*
By Australia out of Disney, or that light plane from
Connemara Regional Airport with its Special Offer of
A 'Return from Anywhere' should that be where you
Choose to start from, longest way round shortest home.

I saw it start that summer of '69 prospecting for a runway
And now it makes a short way home in planes of light
Exquisite as any then that cast their spell across the evening
That fateful summer of unrest on Derry streets, written
On walls no one then could read from far-off Inis Mór
Itself hand in hand with poverty and hand to mouth:

Most of all exports in her lading, summer's big-boned youth.
Even you there, with your suitcase, in your best blue suit,
Wanted by the Gardaí for GBH, slipping aboard like Theoklýmenos,
Who killed a cousin once on an island not entirely unlike this
                                        in Ancient Greece.
Where are you now, I wonder, where did your days wash up
Since I aided and abetted your escape that heart-rent morning?

I never saw it start and will not see it end but to my dying day
Naomh Éanna in your name more than any other let me pray
Sailing down the breakers' yard on the highest winter tide
For those in peril: all who may fail to find their love at last
Returned at such an hour as this the island ushers in
Where all the elements make landfall, here and now, at once

The day long. Though pleasure's nothing without the long
Shadow to which it is the silver lining briefly unfurled and furled
Like an ensign, a national flag even, in a gaunt dawnlight,
As when I saw them in the Sound, the Irish Navy sinister and fleet
Come out of nowhere, the Corvette *Cliona* firing a round
To intercept the Brittany trawler *Gars de la Pointe*

Unlawfully fishing in Irish territorial waters (fined £20.00
In Galway Court). I am the Ireland they're fighting for,
They might claim could they have claimed to speak for Inis Mór.
But who'd make so bold in any court, by Guinness or by god,
Among you, unconversant cousins of the Sicilian O'Mertás,
O'Kosans and MacCalors, locked in your sad vendettas? Still?

What will I find among you now? Memories as sharp as my own
In which I figure merely as the dimmest recollection, even to myself,
Lost soul pilgrim playboy in the wilderness in love with seascapes
And fish-hooks? Escapes and wish-lists? O dear Tom and Margaret,
Should I find you living, all that, and time, will fold into the moment
As when eyes or palms meet in greeting or in parting or in prayer.

O steady witness, *Naomh Éanna*, mute ferry of how many dooms,
Tides and weathers, fair days and foul, with your high prow
And low saloon: when that last time lands for making good escape,
May I come over the island's shoulder and find you and
                                        the others waiting,
Straining at the pierhead, and cattle loading to propitiate the gods,
And a course set never to make landfall anywhere but here again.

(iii) *Cuckoo* (Cuculus canorus)

    Bungowla, Inishmore, 22 May 2000

Those binocular vowels O O
With which from drystone walls
You spy the land and play
The two stops of your double life
Otherwise so singular:

Pipping pipits to the post,
Dunning dunnocks for a down-payment,
What is it with you
On your short wings, like
A hawk at dusk?

O O only turn coins over at
Your bidding and nothing
Want from May to May,

Is comfort I suppose to those
Who like to play away?

Who've written you out of any
Truth and into their feeble guilt,
As if those zeros were lenses
In opera glasses trained
On Don Giovanni.

But tonight around this
Drystone filigree on air
As delicate as any sung,
All turned to light, I hear
The pair of you in stereo

Begun: whirring and purring,
In frenzied ecstasy.
Something else, as they say, worth
Keeping to yourself: O sing,
Cuckoo, and louder, sing.

(iv) *A Tune for Blind Sound*

Some new-wave band into synaesthesia?
In those days nothing of the kind
Would have entered my mind
Tuned as I was to wave-bands more like
Windrows in Sonny's meadow then,
Down where fastidious mullet
Fished the weed and flotsam
And mackerel stormed at the point,
All summer as the tide turned and
Crept round the clock of my fate.

But what if I'd known then what
I know now? Would I have smiled?
Would I have wept? Would I have
Waved on ahead, and cried: Wait for me!
I may not know what I'm doing
But you'll find it has meaning for you
By the time you catch up with me,
For by then that's the way it'll go:
With the tide turned and
The clock fast that was slow.

(v) *A Letter Home: In Memory of the Corncrake*

Kilronan, 23/4 May 2000

I've just blown in and the word seeps out
like rain puzzling the window with
a jigsaw view, bumpy and blurred.
I quartered off whole acres of stone
and sea this afternoon and then met
Tom himself, come riding down
on a mountain bike, behind his collie.
He's seventy-six, still keeps a pony
and some cattle, his eye just a little
rheumy, but his back still straight. I
puzzled him all right, balding and
burlier than the playboy ever looked to become.

After so long there's everything
and nothing to be said. The roll-call
of the dead, who married whom,
how many kids they had. He keeps
the same regime but hasn't taken drink
these past six years. Poor Margaret
had a stroke but is now improving.

Her memory not good. Next morning
with a sickle he went cutting briars,
foursquare methodical, as I remember him,
in his peaked cap, making a cock of each clump.
He didn't look up as I passed; his
buff gardening gloves, a telling sign
how much those times are past.
But nothing's missing to my mind
or his. He lives to a philosophy,
on what he knows is borrowed time,
working as he always did, but when
he leaves these days, he takes the plane,
as when he dies he'll go to heaven.

I worry what we're going to do for talk.
There are gaps here in the evening.
There always were, you know, but not
gaps into which I did the talking.
Gaps in walls. Gaps, though now
the dead outgrow the plot, and that's
with two men lost at sea:
Mikey McDonough, Brian O'Flaherty,
aboard *The Lively Lady*.
They searched the Sound for days.
I said there's nothing missing but
nothing concentrates the mind so
absolutely as to speak too soon.
Some pieces strangely seem to travel.
Facts meet where they didn't before.
And grief has its day once more.

It wouldn't stop raining that night
and the cuckoos wouldn't stop calling,
until gone ten and eleven o'clock.

I've never heard the like. But no more
than ever I could, could I keep indoors,
rain or no rain, boots or no boots (not
quite): I walked out like a gentleman, in
gore-tex coat and over-trousers,
poking the road with a stick,
a rare vagrant passing through,
going up and down, and round about,
from dune to cliff, from bay to Sound,
in the dark: a jig-saw on a loopy circuit,
as the fine rain fell and rinsed the rocks
and filled the air with pungent scent
of seaweed. I thought it was only
a matter of time, and so it was
underneath, before I'd hear one
marching to that old crex crex.
But all I heard was a silence that grew
the more I heard it, until it drowned
everything, drowned all the world,
silenced the whole Atlantic shore, like
a stopped clock, and no one I met
could remember when, how long ago,
the spring failed, as if one evening,
of old age. They were expected but
they didn't come and life is different.

Marcus driving in his trap to meet the boat
all down a dazzled morning, salt-breeze
and sun, high drift of cloud, stops for me
and takes me to Kilronan, by the low road,
for the longer *craic*, of this and that:
Marcus the Roman, Roman name and nose,
but Hector and Achilles in one, those days,
bare-knuckle pugilist, King of the West,

now in round sixty-three, up against age,
who'll take him the distance.
Wild, wild Marcus, who loved his Guinness
but it's no more black stuff, either, now.
Doctor's orders, until the world goes dark.
Graduate from fisherman to jarvey
(classic progress), with stints between,
in Birmingham and the Isle of Grain,
he'll take Yanks for a ride all summer,
telling them the old old story. He's
humoured how the commonplace fascinates
them : 'There's a water tank,' he points,
a corporate umbrella handy, in the event
of rain, 'There's another water tank… We do say,
but sure, we're not interested in them.
We see enough of them, like,' he grins.
Seals play in the ebb below Mainistir and
sea-birds in the air, everywhere perform
at the borders of the picture, where
the blue pieces of sea and sky seem
interchangeable, as life for death,
in a dream departure to unknowing.

As on my final morning. The harbour
in a bustle, and Mourteen having
searched each day to catch me, stops
in his red van on the causeway.
O causeway to what ending? I
can see the youth in the man yet,
father with a family, skipper now,
rival to the Spaniard, in and out of Killibegs.
What's the fuss? (The mini-bus jarveys
are on their mobiles.) Everyone's in it
for once, as all the fishing boats make ready

to sail in convoy out to escort in
the *Shauna Ann*, deep-sea addition to the fleet,
first new boat since…? none could
remember when. Not surely, I thought,
since the *Ard Aengus* (grounded and
wrecked near Glassin Rocks in '68)?
Out they sail beyond Straw Island
and bring her home, under an
arch of flares, in the grey easterly morning.
The women shrill like gulls, the jarvies
sound their horns, as she comes to berth,
some old enactment surviving, flipside of grief.
But there now the *Draoícht na Farraige*,
and no more my love the *Naomh Éanna*,
strains to be gone. And so once more,
in the quick linking of wave into wave,
to the last piece of horizon, I begin to scrawl again
      WITH LOVE, THE END

(vi) *Clearance*

    i.m. Annie Hernon

It is too late for some things,
No use arguing with that.
I should clear my head here now
As one day they cleared out
Stuff beneath the roof in that
Old store: spinning wheel,
Loom (engines of the fates),
Dresser, and drift nets.

But the wind off the Atlantic's
Not enough it seems, nor all

Its glare, like new whitewash,
Narrowing eyes, as when
She smiled. Now she's closed
To everything, like an answer,
Who always shrewdly kept you
Guessing what she thought.

(vii) *Porridge*

Putters softly in the pot like a horse
Trotting down the island in the dawn.

Pan grates at the hob, shoe to road, as we wait.
And round the bleary eye a sleep of oat-film dries.

Rims of the barrow grind, their spokes mill,
Round and round, as we turn.

Light shines bright as grain in the cold air.
Ring of hooves now and husks of late stars.

The sea ripens, shoal upon shoal for harvest,
And we're off to a good start, memory lined again.

(viii) *To the* NAOMH ÉANNA

found rusting in Charlotte Quay, 26 May 2000

Lost among the Dublin quays I found you lost and might not
had I not been lost, by chance, and late about to miss my sailing.
I was your lover once but turned and lost you in the crowd
of stormy seas, and skies too strong for gulls, that day you stood me up
in wild November. They said you'd gone to Dublin then
for a Board of Trade survey. I accepted there were other
men in your life, in every port, and hit the drunken skies by trawler.
But this time, lost in my thirty-year-long labyrinth, and quays,
and old warehousing, and far from thinking of you, I turned and,
suddenly: I saw you, up against the wall. The eye is forever young.
I knew you. For proof I had a camera. But my camera had no film in.
I had to fly or miss my sailing. This was a fleeting fate who else
could share in, now, among the living, and fathom to its end,
and call to mind such sailing we had known, of waves and seabirds
at coming home or leaving: circumlunar, making headway as
making love, on any B or C sailing: out via the islands or
via the islands returning? I knew you, at first sight, unnamed,
through all decay, my sight so young. But we've no hope of ever sailing
now, unless aboard a poem like this, at the harbour wall,
already rusting, and both of us too late for it: not sailing, just listing,
in a basin. Dank reflection, off Pearse Street, and all Dublin
sailing past us as we fail, the breeze in your rigging frail
compared with those Atlantic gales, when the islands
heaved at their mooring, and your high prow so proud,
pitched prouder than ever, in the brunt of the weather,
that I cannot quite believe my eyes I ever saw you, then or now.

DULYN

i.m. Trevor and Ivor, and John

To fish there you wade in air among
The rocks angling for your balance.

Black water chops ashore and the torrent
Holds you bubble-rapt in its sound-warp

Like a dipper submerged in a rushing pool
Intent on caddis larvae.

If one of the others came by to know
Your luck he could startle you to death.

Ghosts as they are, or not. They haunt here
Like the stories they told of ones that got away.

The steep cwm will catch your cast more
Than ever those wily fish might rise before you

To a hook ripped of its barb on a rock.
I learnt in this place, from the age of ten,

To curse like a man, 'God damn it to hell,'
To brew tea in a smoke of heather stalks and downfall,

To tie instant bloodknots and a noose
Round the neck of the Bloody Butcher

While the fish moved out of range
As now that world has veered forever

And every finger's a thumb, my reading glasses
Beaded with rain, and not a fish to be seen.

from PLATO'S AVIARY II

> *'The Admiral knew that the Portuguese had discovered most of the islands in
> their possession by observing the birds.'*
> Christopher Columbus, *Log Book*, Sunday 7 October 1492

(iii) PEREGRINE (*Falco peregrinus*)

All day fishing there I waited as much for its shrill *kek-kek-kek-kek
kek-kek* and scimitar soaring overhead as for the dimpling fish below.

How the day might drift on otherwise, the water hypnotic,
Light falling like manna, and all slap-happy in the rocks.

Every plane and facet of wave-mirror and cliff-hanging
Edge of expectancy, pitched there, in and out of the dream.

What sense trying to address the future? Whatever it contains
Won't include us. The art of waiting its métier as mine.

Once as we came back on an autumn evening, weary for the road,
School to face in the morning, homework not done, down one raced

In his scholar's gold rim glasses, and tear-smudged eye from too
                                                        much study,
And thumped a grouse into the heather. Then, wings winnowing

And alarmed *kek-kek* for cry, it shot away, leaving us its prey,
The bird warm where we found it, severed from its head.

How much out of ten might I get for that? At fourteen, mind-wandering,
Learned only in the progress of the clock, in a world beyond time.

(iv) GOLDFINCH (*Carduelis carduelis*)

Still in these wild places, where
Scarce a human ever comes, they startle up
On sight, and wheel away, twittering and
Wheezing, smokily, buoyed up, like
Down, to land a meadow and a half away,
And flit among the starry thistleheads.

How you would prefer them to delay,
But in some earlier incarnation, I suspect,
They learned to distrust a species that
Will stoop to anything for gold: as those who
With pliers poised among the dead tweaked
Dental fillings out, as if by second nature.

(vi) GREY WAGTAIL (*Montacilla cinereal*)

for Bernard

First one must stand
Where the heart belongs,
Never missing a beat?
Harder to do than you think?
So I was writing when
You flew into my head:
Another favoured spot
In your varied habitat.

Elusive upstream or in
Grey town square, quietly:
Your wing's exquisite waterline,
Your nom de plume, your
Cardiometer tail, blinking,
Where puddle meets sky:
Neither grey nor yellow,
Neither here nor there.

(x) HERON (*Ardea cinerea*)

It is impossible to exclude you from the ark of birds,
Though you stand far back in stillness of how many aeons?

However early we must rise to catch you, reflecting
On the flooding world, with tireless gaze.

However few fish there are to go round and however
Unsociable you are. When the waters reach

The topmost spindly branches where you wade on air and flap
Beside your nest, screeching and screaming defiance:

However you make the hair stand up on the backs of our necks
As if we remembered a time when we knew the perils of
                                        amphibious life

More intimately, we will lower the boat and row to meet you
Our belled oars labouring in wind and rain.

(xi) Y WENNOL (Swallow *Hirundo rustica*)

i.m. R.S. Thomas, d. 25 September 2000

That when sound in you migrates to my tongue,
Now you are gone and the sky turns wintry.

We can't say that we saw you leave.
But suddenly the skies are bare and soon the trees.

In any language the word for absence is empty
But of what we need time to tell.

Nothing I know, from the way I'll always see you
Skimming the hay-meadow in westerly light

After however many thousand miles have fallen
To your sickle and still you wheel and dart

Declaring to the skies one makes a spring
Forever, forget summer and winter in the heart.

(xiv) PHEASANT (*Phasianus colchicus*)

Comes under the wall where it's broken, onto the road:
Humble not a word for him, though; nor his gait

In his scaly crocodile party shoes walking
Delicately on his toes like an elderly gent with corns.

But so burnished, Oriental in his princely ornament,
So finely beaten, his dark copperware

Laced like damascene, with the black rim tip
Indent of the craftsman's hammer mottling

His waistcoat-breast. How well he has worn the night
Down all these years, a thousand and one years exiled,

Out late and looking for the way home, his majesty
In all his finery, still dressed for the banquet, at dawn.

(xviii) ONE FOR THE ROAD

  for Patrick

Visiting my notebook once again,
A notebook smudged and worn:

I find a place where the corncrake still
Goes at it with his sharpening stone

And rusty shears beside the road as if
He has time on his side of the wall.

NOW, THEN

Wake early for an early start and softly
while the world sleeps tight go where

the first of day begins and dawn-light
throws a loop around the nursing air

of some old song you have to heart but
guard well that space between you and

the chorus and only to your self attend:
step up, now then, and sing undaunted.

from ARBORETUM

> *'The subject is very difficult, and the Irish ollaves had no interest*
> *in making it plain to outsiders.'*
> Robert Graves

(i) SILVER BIRCH (*Betula pendula*)

As if seeded from the Northern Lights
and the ghostly watermarks of wilderness,
haunt of bears and wolves, it stands here
almost too bright to believe, at the year's end,
knee-deep in winter's carnage where
rusted bracken hoards a trove of leaf-mould:
O material light, like a painter's impasto
flaked at the edge of brush- or knife-stroke...

So sight floods to a halt in it and thickens
each forsaking minute with last leavings
drained from December's ditch and sky,
like something almost lost to memory
brought to mind: enough to hold me here,
to see the stars sown early like spring wheat.

(v) ROWAN (*Sorbus aucuparia*)

No doubt but your one foot holds
all hope there is for you,
high in that cleft of shadow-substance
where the ouzel sings to the torrent's dance.

So I remember and am attached to you
and that bird, earthed to the voltage of its song,
as I stand uprooted, in this suburban garden,
with a hand around you cursing my luck.

(vi) ASH (*Fraxinus excelsior*)

You're cold as the east wind this morning but I stand in with you
and huddle here for shelter as if those black pyramidal points

at your branch tips rattling the sky's window still hold
heat in their embers and the spirit of spring is already jetting

invisibly to ignite April with your slender flowers. They say
your roots run down as deep as your branches reach skyward.

I have read how the first branch of a maiden ash might
cure all ills and who am I in middle life in middle England

this winter's morning now to doubt it? All balancing acts require
at least an element of faith. So with the squall's passing I

gamely swing my stick and prod the road for home, desperately
trying to remember every ash I've known and every April wood.

(vii) HAWTHORN (*Crataegus monogyna*)

So hedged about as you are with omens and
legends, how can I ever hope to break through,
to see you unburdened of everything, except
spring blossom or starkly criss-crossed winter light,
when your Christ's crown, your May catalogue
of antiseptic bridal wear, become you so well?
And your Lear-on-the-heath bad-hair-day blows
my mind to see you in the cold blast blown? Or

I feel I've stared too hard into a Jackson Pollock
and thrown a fit and found myself coming to
on the dark side of a late Beethoven quartet,
played on a seventy-eight, with one of your thorns
for a needle, as I've heard said can be done?
How on earth can I ever hope to see you,
wood for trees if not timber for timbre? Well,
in two successive gardens now, I've planted
you and nurtured, and entered into your being,
like a wren or a robin or sudden song-thrush
going in and out, unscathed, or briefly singing,
and stood to savour you, at all points of the
thorny compass, in blossom and fruit and leaf-fall.
And as you know there are evenings when I've
softly closed my hand about your shank, and
stirred you round and round, as I've been told
will radiate down to the outposts of your root-tree
and give them firmer hold in the underworld,
and never harm came of it, not a scratch, nor
a penny the poorer have I been, but *au contraire*
I've thrived and revelled in your growing.

(x) IVY (*Hedera helix*)

Be silent unless you have something
better than silence to say.

(xii) HOLLY (*Ilex aquifolium*)

Whoever worked to cut the template for your leaves
pricked his finger, as you know, and drew a bead of blood.

He was rehearsing for the greater project of the stars:
his life's work, you might be tempted to suppose.

But believe me, it's the same old story: the best effects
arrive as if from nowhere in the mind the mind has been before.

Truth stands where it is seeded. As here at the wood's border
your crown at evening holds against the sky the first stars I
ever saw.

(xiv) WHITE POPLAR (*Populus alba*)

Today, October turns and turns
your shoals dark and light, in a flood of air.
The rain blowing from you reminds me
of the showers of pollen a season ago
that filled the air to gasping for air.

The wind runs and runs and the leaves
cannot quicken any longer in your branches
so fly faster through the rain's fine spray,
blown along the air like giant pollen
in flurries, the air itself gasping for air.

The tree of old age, they say. But even
Hercules might die today for want of breath,
staring at aspens through a windswept window.
Not everyone can say they own trees,
said the old man suddenly, in revelation.

Yesterday he'd struggled on his stick
and dragged a plastic chair a hundred yards
the better to survey them, breathless
on a day of such autumnal stillness
not a leaf stirred or fell to earth.

(xvi) WILLOW (*Salix viminalis*)

'Burn not the willow, a tree sacred to poets.'

Beware the soft hand-shake. It is
the mark of one whose mind is elsewhere.

A supple heart is strongest of all
for weaving withies into fish-traps.

Ancient sayings from the poetics
of the workshop for the blind.

(xviii) YEW (*Taxus baccata*)

But what a pretext for reflection this,
a mouthpiece for the dead, a root to each
pair of lips. In the old lore 'yew' and 'I'
both stood for death, you know? Death,
then, is evergreen and in the pink, as in
your strong and supple limbs, your
darkest leaves and small red fruit, with which
you've cast a shadow for so long across
this limestone corner of the countryside.

For what? To assist us in our melancholy?
Or just so that a skulking blackbird might
pause to sit and gaze a thousand years
while you bring light to dark like this and
dark to light the silence of your song?

BELONGING

Who put the longing into it?
The longing to leave so that
We might belong in longing
To return again, and again?

Who put the being into it?
The being that is never the same
So that when we come back to it
All we have is a name?

ALLT

lines from an Autobiography

All through the night the tide
roared on the air, roared in
the trees and soughed about
our steady stone-built, slate
-roofed house, Tan-yr-allt
'under the wooded hill':
where we slept in the roof
as near heaven as we could
though not as near the stars
as the wild allt itself but
in middle-earth above the coast,
borderers in every sense
(M^{c}s not aps), between sea
and mountain, sleeping dream
and waking, under the
foundering air: all through
the night, ar hyd yr nos.

Ar lan y môr... Not just dreams
either but faith also, though of
no formal kind for us. When they
sang in that school hall 'There is
a Green Hill Far Away...' my
clock-watching mind's eye
saw no Christ but Eden's
wind-bent bluff blowing
gorse and hawthorn, larch
-scrub in limestone outcrop,
nestling violets, gentians, cowslips,
every kind of bird and
springtime egg, jackdaws
cackling, ravens going cronk
and back-vowelled gulls
bobbling and keening, guttural
fulmars, all riding high as
hope above the town.

And sitting here idling at six
of a morning (in Massachusetts),
my head spins as if years were
altitude and all my travails had been
to climb them, and find myself
turned inside-allt again, clinging
by my fingertips, reaching for
a gull's egg breakfast...
As if I might begin to make
meaning of my lot now in that
cold morning then, above the
town, summer coming in
(as now) from England's last
satanic mills, for donkey-rides,
punch and crocodile, deck-chairs

between downfall... Happy Valley.
Whistling in the dark until
autumn shut up shop and
banged and rattled into winter.

And left us to it, as I'm left to it
here, haunted by that place:
whistling in the dawn, scribbling
to make sense of those gaping
wide-eyed days, yielding and
unyielding. Still unfallen,
I never looked down on
anything then, but looked both
down and up, longing from
that fastness, atop a lane as
rocky as a mountain (mind's
rough road to climb again).
And looked away from lessons
and the law, back into my
heart's dark wood, distracted
as I grew, and grew weary
and wary to embrace expulsion,
already by then pen-in-hand,
digging word-bait, hooking bass...

A tale since washed overboard,
writing the lives of fish, and birds:
I spy with my little eye something
beginning... as I strode out at ten
-years-old, TUF-booted then hobnailed,
lost and found, under the high
Carneddau... from first of March
to the last of September, fishing;
at sixteen fingered by the poets

and fatefully fired into orbit
like Sputnik over Snowdonia
by Thomas & Thomas & Co.,
Graves, Hopkins, MacDiarmid,
Lawrence, Kavanagh, Synge…
whirled slowly round their wheeling
word-warp rhyme-realm, until,
one November drunk and
sober I made my re-entry
and fell to earth on Inis Mór.

And stayed there and felt
at home in that limestone
landscape, sea-rocked at
the edge of the world,
though scarce a tree to be heard there
but the sound of a tumultuous wood
heard everywhere, at sea in the
driftwood flotsam-jetsam
deciduous Atlantic…

Our allt was no Eden like that,
but a once-formal garden, then
wilderness: corner of a small estate
that fell to us, the villa of some
Roman (captain hotelier) run to
ruin and rendered barbarous,
preferred above humbler Coed Coch.
We occupied his gardener's lodge
and lived walled off from Rome,
not citizens and, if natives, not
descendants but outsiders.

Behind high walls topped with
valerian: rabbits in the nettles,
geese one time beneath the wood
stood sentry at the western gates,
cats gone feral, foxes for wolves;
a sundial that told no time in
Roman numerals, and honey
in the hive, a vinery under glass
with antique iron heating ducts
(deep tanks, one sunken, like
a Roman bath unearthed) in rack
and ruin, though bearing fruit
grapes for a Welsh elegy, drunk
under towering nordic pines
that swayed and staggered overhead
dizzying the windswept stars,
their cones clustered stars.

They stood in phalanxes above
the courtyard and up the side of
Fferm like props on the frontier
in a movie called 'The Last Days
of Marcus Aurelius'. And yet
in summer-light those trees
were pure Mediterranean: their
trunks, oyster-shell edged, orange-
pink-grey, impossible pastels, black
damascene lace-maps. Their cones
clicked open in the heat or
clattered down (our winter kindling)
to rest on beds of needles and
grasses where grasshoppers
hopped and thrushes bathed in
dust and tawny shafts of sun.

Allt... one of the oldest words,
older than any English word?
(But halt and prick your ears
along the marches to hear holt.)
And young now on every native
childhood's tongue, almost as though
Rome had never been or England's
empty empire. At John Bright
Grammar School (neither ysgol nor
radical but patronising pseudo-
Arnoldian), we did not learn and
learnt the lie of the land. What
the eye doesn't see the heart
can't grieve over, and we didn't
grieve, nor do I now. But what
wonders in that wild place the
heart might miss a beat to tell.

Each morning as I brushed my teeth
I looked out on Bryn Maelgwyn,
bardic allt, on Llanrhos and Deganwi:
landmarks in the Mabinogi where
pouting Taliesin sang and blerwm,
blerwm babbled back his rivals
blerwm, blerwm... Barbaric Welsh
to Roman ears, to Latin ears and
Anglo-Saxon: allt where I skulked,
the mind's allt to which those
reticent hicks called Prytherch,
Llewelyn and ap Rhys Owen
retreated, biding their time, cannily
keeping their counsel in the
dark wood of their tongue.

M^c maybe I am but what ish
my nation? I was born there…
Yet no man, as Taliesin said,
sees what supports him. So
soon I went, eager to leave
and not incapable of leaving.
Though back I came within a year:
O dark wood, O allt unaltered,
to leave, and leave again for home
(from America, the short way now).

IN VINO VERITAS

The wires ran straight
like a stave to hold a tune in line.

But the vine wove its own
design as if to prove it could.

With leafy grace notes and trilling
tendrils it composed itself.

So learn how to hold your drink
and find your own way home.

AT ROUNDSTONE

for Tim Robinson

At Roundstone the tide was in,
making its peace with the moon.
Night clambered aboard and the air
filled with sea-sound and bird-cry,

as if making headway for… let's not
say where: but the heart knows its
harbour, registered there and still
fishing, with torn net and star-haul
blowing bright as the March light
that we stopped en route to stalk
to its source, down a bay of coral
whose name I've forgotten, vanishing
in the biting wind that blew there,
before we made it darkling to your board.
And you and I and Máiréad had
only to smile and laugh on meeting,
like long-lost comrades (or a conclave
of corncrakes, grinning), so much had
that island meant, looked for
and unlooked for, every square inch
of the heart, beyond measure.
But all we ever wanted is meaning,
to note the finest nuances of stone
and light and how they map
themselves and map us. For meaning
regarded as an end of desire,
as another island-haunter said,
is value, as found, for example,
in the hypnosis of repetitive days
(your phrase), and must itself be
charted, fractal by fractal, and
converted word for word, minutely
into words, page by Lilliputian page,
to show what this world has endured
and lost, and would have lost
the more (time out of mind)
but for your finding your vocation
ever to hand around stone and sea
unfolding and folding landscapes.

AMERICAN WAKE

Heading for America, on St Stephen's evening,
A vision from below swam up to haunt me:
The islands in the bay's mouth, gliding.
The day was turning thin, no sign of habitation,
From that height, or hint of colouration, yet
From the cast of light I knew, if one asked there,
'Will it rain?', the question was her answer.
It seemed a miracle to me that I should see them:

I never take a window seat (to speed escape
On landing) but stood up just to stretch my legs,
And by some gift or grace of timing, glimpsed
Them, through a port-hole: the parting glass,
Raised between us, and since who must go, and who
Must stay? the moment made me wonder.

PLOUGHS

We wheel with the gulls.

We weep clods.

We toil between harvests
or lounge among nettles.

We do not keep our nose clean.

THE BLACKSMITH'S ORDER CENTENARY

*An elegy in memory of John McNeillie 1865–1941
and of John McNeillie 1916–2002, to be read aloud.*

*From Clarksburn Smithy, Portwilliam, to Mr John McCallam,
Clachaneasy, Newtonstewart*

*Sir please Send me acknowledgement
of Scrap Mettel, supplied to you I sent off
on November 30th and also the balance
or whatever it may be until we have
the account squared up as I want that done
until I get my order sent in for some
plough mettels this year in time and
also send me price of what you can
supply plough Boards and soles and
landsides per cwt for this season
I want to make a little alteration on
my patterson plough Broad this year
and You will oblige John McNeillie*

O I would oblige you, John McNeillie,
hammering at my key Broad here
(the thing we call spellchecker fails)
thinking of your soles and landsides,
your plough mettels… (Microsoft
furrows underneath in red: 'landsides'
and 'mettels'), and that little alteration,
as who would not make if he could?
And see us meet the day on 22 July,
a hundred years away from here, or there,
at nettle-deep rusty Clarksburn Smithy,
this very summer, as it would be? And

what might we not say, by the cwt, together?
(I've often dreamt... and dream still.)
How little future there is in any thing?
And you would know who built to last.
What past the world might care to know?
Technologies of how to make a plough
Broad, patterson or no, or word-processor?

Who said the plough is immortal?

The constellations are as far from me as you,
their sparks hanging fire in God's ruined smithy.
But in your house my father grew,
and we are close, as he was close to you.
And when I look him in his eye it is
an eye you looked into, and when I shake
his hand a hand you shook and shook
a blackened smithy with your clout until
sparks flew like gulls behind a plough
(as Darwin drew). As words would fly,
if I could strike things right, until we had
the account 'squared up', whatever it may be.

And that still shakes me through: that
little span we might have closed, handful
of years to weigh against your mettel. There's
scrap here too in my 'waste bin' by the ton.
So now I toil and sweat to melt it down
and hammer out lines, in your memory,
rugged enough for any stony field.
I've longed for such a meeting since a boy,
in some hereafter where we might be 'men':
the old man, you, and me, together...
with a bottle of Bladnoch to hand...

Little I thought to hear from you by letter
but here I find you folded neat inside
an envelope, roughly 5x3.5, addressed to
Clachaneasy, and sent it seems by hand,
to 'The Crown Implement Works' or
so you scrawled, on 22 July 1901,
regarding yours of 30th November.

Here fog billows down the Bladnoch,
my hand slips… my glass briefly
out of kilter with my lips, and Bladnoch
in her meadows grows sombre like the Styx.

Time never deals in sentiment: it doesn't give a damn
for little alterations or the balance of our lives
or witness or… any of our loyalties (or dis-)….
but from Dis to Disneyworld and farther,
to you and to that other John I'll drink
however much it takes to loose a tongue,
so we might lose and find ourselves again.
At some belated date somehow our tribe
moved from the iron age to the age of scribe,
blacksmith to wordsmith, mettel to paper.
God knows how. Except by 'God' himself,
read in the Bible; and story-telling at your hearth:
of rackrenter Maxwell, and 'mighty men'
of Mochrum, McFee some Irish kin of ours…
tales from the forge, politics of the smithy,
and those books you bought at house sales.
Rabbie Burns, kenned inside oot, and…
Dryden's Virgil? You a man believed in
devil's imps and fairies (Brownyis and
Bogillis), your life closer to 'Tam O'

Shanter', ever than to me? Your labour
never any kind of 'eclogue', Virgilian or other?

Dryden? The one the old man cut his teeth on:
half-schooled first ever writing John McNeillie,
on whom you doted, your pride the prodigy,
author of 'harum-scarum' *Wigtown Ploughman*,
quoted, for all its scandalous swearing, from
the pulpit in the churches of Wigtown,
Portpatrick, Kirkmaiden, Mochrum, Sorbie...
that boy who 'ran about half naked'
now 'shure to do some good to others'?
For that is where he 'shone in waking up
and showing the publick, the houses
and conditions people lives in... the unwashed
ploughmen tribe, born of Divels imps or
poison wasps, led by the divel himself...
cot folks without education or caracter,
only lives for day, and daily bread, and
a fight or a quarl, after thay have thair
bely full, and gets thair tail up...' I quote
your letters at you as you wrote, in English,
though you lived and thought in Scots.

Word-shod together we'll wear longest of all?
So I'll melt your words into my own
and speak on paper as to the first I meet:
just as you told a story... Until I find you
past your last winter, and Hitler rampant:
'let him spin the rope that will hang him'
the end of a tow 'the safest place for a madman',
his ploughshares turned to bombs and tanks;
and you write 'Dear John a few lines to say'
how the world was all that time away,

last lines from you, last from your hand,
amen (I quote from your distress to reap
what comfort?) '...now getting scarce of fodder,
trashed out the last stack and now only two
small stacks of hay, and no sign of grass.
So we are almost on the verge of want,
and money cant get it, so thare we are,
coming on to starvation with losing half
of the turnips with the frost and snow...'

22 July 2001

FATHER AND SON

There's strength in silence, he said,
Looking across at me for emphasis.
The more you say the more malleable
You become. I slipped out on some
Excuse and wrote it down. We'd whisky
In us and my heart foresaw a poem.

Then I sat there gazing, as if through
A window, glazed by the dram. And the view
Stayed me, and I sat silent. And,
If you tell your offspring, he resumed,
Your grandchildren, anything about them:
Tell them what good men they were.

Whose reputation and for what
Are we weighing here, my heart
Faltered? But firmly now,
As if by calculation to forestall...
He gestured at the anaesthetic, and
So I poured and we both drank.

ONE MORE TIME

By now his outdoor orbits of the house
approach the frequency of comets passing.

Yet when I ask what he's been up to since
he says he's been out in the fields walking.

And at once I know where he means. He says
he goes to keep his mind from wandering.

PRAYER

Bless those who are marginal, who only live.

Bless those whose motto is *il faut cultiver ton rêve*.

Bless those who know what lies behind the times.

AN ORIENTAL TALE

from 'The Clutag [formerly Sycamore] Press'

The machine has Josiah Wade, Halifax, Eng.,
stamped on its great cog, and 'ARAB' in its arch.

Even the black one-eyed stare of its ink-disk
helps serve the telling of an oriental tale

from Victorian Britain. Here I add to it, letter by
letter, setting a poem from the bottom up.

It reads from right to left. But then, it's true,
everything in this world is back to front.

The art lies in turning it front to back.
So I pray in my garage to a small dark god.

HALF A LOAF

A poem like life's a half-way house though
nothing can be halved that's not complete.

Half a loaf's better than no bread. A crumb of wisdom
finds a world, in a grain of wheat.

The tortoise steals for ever on the hare
while Zeno cuts a cake that isn't there.

God knows we shall be forced into retreat
and live our days out on thin air.

A WATCHED CLOCK

The clock once stood above a Scottish fire.
Ticking and chiming, it tolled for a world too
Busy to hear it. But still they kept observance round it,
As if it was the eye of god. Now it ticks away for us,
An antique, with a little pendulum, imported
From America: THE KENMORE made in
Connecticut by the Ansonia Clock Company, 1878.

On its face, the old man has inked in names
And dates of our tribe, spidery ghosts under glass.
He ticks them off like an assiduous obituarist,
With anecdotes. As who, in time, will tell of him?
The key to his heart's so worn now it will not
Turn the spring. But once again it's time to go. I look
Into his eye, and rising say: 'Goodbye, until…'

AT WALDEN POND

The finger-post pointed through the trees
Like a moment in a poem by Robert Frost.
The direction was as straight as any but
I might be walking yet and not have found it,
Or where, precisely, it once stood. I stopped,
And turned away to look down at the pond.
There a canoe of Indian design, unreal, lay
Like halves of a pea-pod, joined seamless
At the waterline: two fishermen as one fished
In two ponds. Everything in Walden woods
That day, in Walden pond in Walden sky
Swam in that plumbed blue ether-world,
Collapsing space and direction into light.
I stepped back down to walk the water's edge
And stooping (or was I reaching up?) picked
From the shore a stone, shot through with
Stars of quartz, to carry home, as if to weight
My heart's plumb-line, and bring my feet
Back to the ground, like this. To a house
I built myself, a mile from any neighbour.

THE SHIPWRECK AT CAPE COD

This scene would haunt anyone
capable of feeling: the many
marble feet and matted heads

of 'immigrants' from Galway in 1849:
famine time left unremarked
in Princeton's 'Historical Introduction'.

The drowned look out through
wide-open staring eyes, like dead-lights
or cabin windows filled with sand.

Here and there a bonnet or
a jacket, a woman's scarf, a gown,
decorates the wreck of weed.

Yet undistracted seaweed gatherers
carry off their harvest, drown who might:
why care at all for bodies?

While others cart corpses in
rough deal boxes to a hole
like a cellar: sober despatch

of business, no less moving
to his mind, the sea still
breaking violently on the rocks.

And a little further on her frail
flag spread on a rock to dry,
held down by stones at the corners.

NEAR MYSTIC

The white man comes, pale as the dawn,
With a load of thought, not guessing but
Calculating. Nations are not whimsical.
The Indian does well to continue Indian.
So driving out from Mystic, aptly, I
Pondered some pages I'd been reading.

It was a foggy morning and the woods
Kept eerie track with the road.
Their presence felt, they melted into air,
As once the Pequot must have stalked
The Yengeese. So ghostly was the way,
I nearly missed the sign to the Casino.

HONEYSUCKLE

I bought a trellis to support a vine.
The vine was slow to wind itself
out of the earth and climb.
For several seasons I wondered where
responsibility lay, whether with myself
and want of patience or
poor stock or soil or something on the air.

So I would look from my window
of an idle hour, waiting,
like a prisoner staring out through
his solitary confinement's little grating,
at the course of time.
And the vine still scarcely grew
as if daunted by that trellis frame.

So things went until I took
no care in it, troubling neither to
pluck it out nor study honeysuckle in a book.
And so it grew, and slowly grew
time out of mind and now
trellis and vine embrace, as if,
for all the world, for dear life.

STONES

The stones on my sill hold their cold
ovals and angles steadily, rock steady.

Lodestones to my uprootedness they
anchor me, weigh me up and down, all told,
though I leave out of mind the place
I took them from, for charm and talisman,
for that burden's too full a refrain
ever to be my saving grace.

Mornings I cover them with outspread
hands and feel them numb to the bone,
as if I reached for them in a streambed.
They're as cold, god knows, as ice,
like the gaze of one who has
the measure of you and all you ever said.

IN MEMORIAM VERNON WATKINS (1906–67)

I published a poem in America,
in *Shenandoah*, courtesy of Greer
& Dabney. Of which I remember
nothing, neither title nor idea,
but the image of a magpie ladling light
and dark. I stole *Poetry for Supper*
by R.S. Thomas (the higher hunger)
from a Swansea bookshop, black and white
indeed. Thieving magpie on £5 a week
and penny-a-line. You think I joke? I
sent poems to Vernon Watkins who wrote back
that he never described for its own sake.
Truth's metaphysical beyond the eye.
Then he died. What did he mean, for god's sake?

IN DEFENCE OF POETRY

Older than we are by however many ages,
it doesn't need defending against anything.
No more do air or fire, earth or water.
Not even in our empty times. Neglected, it will
go underground, or into interstellar space.

Until out of the blue someone calls it up,
like the Greek who cut my hair last week.
Where was he from? 'Spar-ta,' he said.
'You are a Spartan!' I exclaimed. 'Oh no,'
he said, 'there are no Spartans anymore.'

THE STATE OF PLAY ON THE RIALTO

These days he haunts me everywhere I go
as even on a mid-life week in Venice,
washed up at the Guggenheim, I notice
La Nostalgie du poète by de Chirico.
It turns me on like the blue note at the bridge
across the Amman, the blind stare's in-
stress inscrutable, as fish or mannequin,
a life lived always elsewhere on the edge.

How could Orpheus with his song and lyre
not look back and quit the race while still ahead
or face the music of his heart's desire?
Not the thing-in-itself but the other

thing-in-itself, haunting shade, alienated,
that is poetry's eternal power?

TO A CRITIC

'Our age prefers a light touch…'
Someone's acquired a plural,
someone's acquired an age.
If it isn't too much trouble
may time prove his scourge.

PORTRAIT OF THE POET AS A YOUNG DOG

for Diana Maureen Porter

(i) *Diana and Actaeon*
This is the subject beyond all others
that once again will turn me upside
down: so Actaeon had no place to hide
and no defence, for all his antlers.
I steel myself to failure just the same
as I did when youthful lust propelled me,
longing for you, whoever you might be,
before I even knew your name.

This is the story that's as old as time
or young as it and writes itself
according to the formulae: sublime
and ridiculous, at once. However
it turns out, happily, or comes to grief,
it is of all of them, forever after.

(ii) *Hume's* Enquiry
Just as I might believe I've signalled my
intention here, so with a longing look
and then another, I turned back from my book
to stare at her, thinking I'd caught her eye,
across the lecture theatre. Hume's *Enquiry*
had no chance against the cause
-and-effect impact of her on my gaze,
and nothing dreamt in his philosophy.

My true Penelope (as the poet said)
wasn't Petrarch's Laura but Zhivago's
Julie Christie, and all the girls from head
to foot her look-alikes in maxi-coats, high boots
(I tell it like it was) and back-combed hairdos.
And all the mophead boys were poets?

(iii) *For the Fallen*
   for John Barnard

Or so they fancied, in their innocence,
in nineteen-sixty-five and -six. But then
'innocence is no earthly weapon',
and they were nothing of the sort. So tense,
lugubrious Geoffrey Hill, reliably
informed them, in the course of lectures on
poetry from Yeats to Hughes and Gunn,
sweating in his funeral suit of charcoal grey.
His black shirt, in that artificial light,
caught tenebrous hues, green as Baudelaire
's dyed hair; his pudgy face so queer,
his brow so damp, as if he spent the night
in hell-on-earth, every day of the year,
and knew he was the only poet there.

(iv) *Esse est percipi*
He was for me at least the only show
in town (Christ, what a pantomime!), except
for Quentin Bell, whose teasing humour kept
'bad art' in the picture, and taught me how
deeply gravity may depend on laughter,
and vice versa. Thoughts on De Gustibus
(tasteless! tasteless!) still make me focus…
on how we cannot read the future.

But it was in philosophy
I could count on the thought that I'd see her.
Esse est percipi opined Berkeley.
Oh don't tell me what I know already:
to be is to be perceived, but would she ever,
or would she never, perceive me?

(v) *A Vision of Reality*
The youth from Wales as silent as the hills,
shore-dweller, mountain-haunter, 's truly
an innocent abroad, however guilty,
lost in that world, for want of social skills.
He dreams and drowns in so much liberty:
Tetley's, John Smith's, Magnet Ales,
the like of which were never sunk in Wales,
or not while gazing on A VISION OF REALITY.

Not her but 'A Study of Liberalism in
Twentieth-century Verse' by Frederick Grubb,
a sort of Lives of the Poets, open
in his lap at Yeats, Eliot, Auden…
Thomas, his worm's eye fiddle and hubbub,
thrown in as if to bring me down.

(vi) *L'Albatros*
It is no sin to lose your way, whatever
price the gods exact, backwoods boy in
the urban night, homesick, courting ruin,
through a glass darkly. Hell or high water,
see him cross the street like an albatross
to catch the last bus back to Lawnswood,
as if he weirdly understood
the path to truth begins in loss.

How else might the heart ever know beauty?
As just a bourgeois entertainment,
good taste converted into booty?
But forget all that... Whenever will he
get to meet her? So between sonnet
and sonnet here, even I begin to worry.

(vii) *Like a Rolling Stone*
On the day he'd betray the girl from home,
he drove with the boys over Ilkley Moor,
in a black Ford Pilot, out looking for
'The Twelve Apostles', singing as they came:
'Hey! You! Get off of my cloud...' Driving
around, from cloud to cloud they sped
up-hill-down-dale until the sky bled
and night closed in about their skiving.

Repairing to the Skyrack and the skite,
he slipped out unobserved, undercover,
awol from the crowd to keep his date.
O dear woman, whatever were you thinking,
as I stole up to be your lover
in best clandestine style for kissing?

(viii) *i.m.* Le Deuxième Sexe
I can still remember the instant when
I sensed her scent, the touch of her,
taste of her mouth, her aura... O daughter
of de Beauvoir... what passion drove you then?
First, never second, sex, you second-guessed
my gaze and asked me nothing in return
but what you gave was all I had to learn
however long it took that we were blessed.

The signs we read or else read us may be
signs of our times that time alone translates.
I see our like now and invisibly pass by,
on the other side. In vain to tell them
their icons are as dust before the Fates,
all hormones and biology the dream?

(ix) *'The Tree' revisited*
But once we've dreamt it, how we can't
help but mourn it? Midnight had them
canoodling in the Hollies, carpe noctem:
Zhivago's Russia had no colder brunt
than that northern winter's starry wind
like a sharp blast blown from Siberia.
So he played Yury to her Lara
and never thought how things might end.

The poems he wrote for her told where
he came from (courtesy of Thomas & Co)
but none the less failed to dissuade her.
As did 'The Tree' which, so he said,
betrays no strength but as the winds blow,
gives, and bides its time, and keeps its head.

(x) *Northern House*
As she at least did. I couldn't say
the same for him, with his sudden antlers
wired-up out through the branching stars,
over the hills and far away
in Wales. There Christmas laboured and,
conscienceless, he relished with delight
the double life; and lay awake at night,
longing for her, with his pen to hand.
O juvenilia! Still they said they'd
do a pamphlet. Somewhere I have proof,
up there, north northwest, inside my head.
That box of vanities beneath the roof,
the place most poems meet their end.
For which give thanks, imaginary friend.

(xi) *In Vaucluse*
   for John Fuller

So late, so soon, the crisis came and time
to pack his bags and books and sling his hook,
a statistic in the failure rate. His look
a fallen angel's. Disgrace and shame
at home heaped on him for his wild folly.
So off he set intent upon his quest
and journeyed to the bottom of the worst,
heart-wounded in Vaucluse, just north of Swansea.

But you know already my dog's leg story.
To those who don't it's hardly gripping news.
What is the end of autobiography?
This ruse to simulate a date with fate,
to try again to best the muse
at some point of no return: so soon, so late?

DEATH

How many times was it those foggy anaesthetic days
when I could hardly see a hand before my eyes but felt your breath?
I've learnt not to look for an intelligent answer from you...
But I remember that break-of-day you stood your ground for once,
as if it was yesterday, and I travelling the low road of my idyll,
knowing this was it at last and he was with you.
Nothing I thought or said could alter that. He'd not stir
if I slipped my hand under the blanket and shook his foot
the way he used to do to me, afraid we might be late
for the morning rise and shine up there in paradise.

How many times but never again like that, not now I know you
for what you are? Like the back of my hand, as they say,
your grip tightening even as it loses hold, has lost its hold
on reason, now on life, as you loiter there as if to be sure this is it.
And what then is it after all but nothing we knew wouldn't happen?
Still I sat on there watching those signs of nothing gather,
as if incredulous. It haunted me for weeks of mourning
I can tell you, dumbly, down all my failure
to love anyone adequately, inadequate to know my feelings
and to make them known. As now I see too late.

SHADE AT THE FUNERAL

This is how I search my wounds:
feeling my pockets from outside.
Patting them to check, for example,
spectacles and verses are to hand.

GONE FOR GOOD

How many more poems will you haunt,
old man? I know you won't say, but
don't pretend you're not keeping count.
I know you and I know you're not done yet.
As on those endless dour days you'd cast
and cast into the evening and keep casting
while I'd pray the next would be your last
not knowing then that faith is everlasting.

My mother said you just upped and left
but that was ever your way, if you could.
Given half a chance to fish I'd do the same.
There's nothing new except we are bereft
and now we say you've gone for good
which so far hasn't lived up to its name.

HEDGE FUND

How they clutch at my heart,
last year's birds' nests
in the mind's bare branches
this New Year's Day.
Stuff in manuscript,
ink-squiggle and thicket.

How long will it weather?
Will it see spring?
With what hope or luck,
refurbishment, revision,
rethreading tweak of the pen
clutch your heart as well?

IN MEMORIAM CAREY MORRIS (1882–1968)

In the clutter of his studio
he made what I took to be trench tea,
leaves in the cup, hot water. No, Tommy
knew no such luxury, oh no...
But those leaves about my gums and teeth
made me gag as if a whiff of gas still
lingered on the air he breathed, enough to kill
a green recruit like me, or hasten death.
But death spared him then. He was a fighter,
this South Wales Borderer of the Slade
and Newlyn schools, a wheezy raconteur,
who told how Edward Thomas would call by,
sit where I sat, with that 'doomed look' he had,
as if already claimed for history.

MEDITATION ON ARMISTICE DAY

In memoriam Corporal Joe Hoyles MM, no. 3697, 13th Rifle Brigade,
B Company

I'll step in here where barely legible advice
to trespassers lies in the ditch, fungus
chewing a corner of it, as if it's starving.
But there's so much to devour here in this
rackety winter wood... I nearly wrote mood,
you'd lose your mind trying to account for it.

The burnt-out house by now almost
metamorphosed into ash-trees, ashes to ashes,
haunting here like Colonel Johnny's ghost.
So I imagine. The mind has forests of them

and true stories that wind through them
like that little burn I once stole along half-scared.

How a place can be a shadow of its former self,
in process of forgetting here. Even the non-biodegradables
that skirt the hedge, the trash of trash, take on
a bloom of dirt and algae, the life of atoms,
microscopic winter spores, clues to death
by a thousand myopic cuts, oozing all away.

The only way out is not through but round?
Like the chainsaw blade and the blue whiff
of two-stroke and resinous dust, to dust. If it were
as easy to tend the mind, with its dead wood
and undergrowth fermenting and fomenting,
I would join the forestry commission's ambulance brigade.

Meanwhile, uncle, the day bends to its task, convex, concave,
it billows light and beats its bounds with
bare branches like lackeys of some old Estate
for towering pheasants where beeches make
a stand and in the hollow the guns volley
as far back as Mametz Wood, where the Welsh went at it.

from GLYN DŴR SONNETS

'The race that is oppressed shall prevail in the end,
for it will resist the savagery of the invaders.'
from 'The Prophecies' of Merlin

(v) *Cynefin glossed*
What is another language? Not just words
and rules you don't know, but concepts too
for feelings and ideas you never knew,
or thought, to name; like a poem that floods
its lines with light, as in the fabled
origin of life, escaping paraphrase.
So living in that country always was
mysterious and never to be equalled.

For example, tell me in a word how
you'd express a sense of being that
embraces belonging here and now,
in the landscape of your birth and death,
its light and air, and past, at once, and what
cause you might have to give it breath?

(vi) *Owain's poetics*
The art is to leave your calling card and
melt away. To keep them wondering what
it is you're up to, haunting the page at
the edge of sense, as if you understand
their dreams. Nature's not the only thing that
can't abide a vacuum, myth also
fills in absence, to make a legend grow.
The past might serve to your advantage but
leave prophecy to Merlin (via Hopcyn...)
And the rest is not silence but history.

Meanwhile keep the door of your mansion
unlocked and your whereabouts a mystery.
And if you will write poetry, then
observe the disciplines, attend to scansion.

(vii) *'Prophecy' from Iolo Goch's Last Poems*
If failure is all you have known, perhaps
you had far better learn to love it as
the blighted seed of promise that it was
than despair entirely? Survive on scraps.
And if the pathos of those near misses,
defeat snatched from the jaws of victory,
afford you solace, like the mystery
in poetry, then make good your losses.

Six hundred years is a long time to wait.
And what you waited for bears no likeness,
not the remotest resemblance, to what
has arrived, or he could begin to dream,
or you have forgotten. None the less,
you do well now to honour his name.

(viii) *9/18/1400*
That autumn morning, out of the wide blue
future, when they razed the town of Rhuthun
to ground zero, how many of them knew
what was afoot? Not even Owain.
Though he would prove as good a strategist
as any of them, from Odysseus
to Osama, from Allah back to Zeus,
the best laid schemes are only so much mist.

So I write here, now, like the lost remnant
of his retinue, or plaid, pursuing
lines of attack on the spur of the moment.
Deluded like most people that I know
enough to be doing what I'm doing
and why on earth I might be doing so.

(ix) *A Monoglot Trout*
First light, in England, travelling westward,
meets me looking for it, up for it at
scraich of innocence again, drop-of-a-hat:
a boy-man rising ten who clambered,
nervous at heart, to look time in the eye,
reticent in simple hope and silence
of loud wilderness: deliverance
that held me captive then, and will until I die.

When the bailiff came and said in English:
'I don't suppose you have a permit?'
Maredydd turned and offered him a fish.
I turned in silence and looked away.
So licence waived for a monoglot trout,
brithyll (in Welsh), we lived to fish another day.

(xxi) *Paradiso: Dulyn, 1957*
It was discipline and fleetness of mind
and footwork in the old metres carried
the day up there, those days bedazzled
by sun and cloud running on the wind.
The poets prolific in all they touched,
quick to hook their lines into the rising

poems, whether at dawn, midday or evening.
They could do nothing wrong. And it seemed

Wales was theirs forever, rain or shine.
No one came up that far but if he did
they knew him without looking twice,
come over the top from nearer heaven
and shared a brew and said, word of god,
they'd find no better day in paradise.

(xxvii) *The Emerald Isle Express*
I knew where you came from before I knew
your destination: see destiny and
nation pun, as if they understand
how poems and railways work. My dreams grew
a network from the moment I looked up,
at your seashore mirrors, shimmying off,
with allure of elsewheres, and promise of
escape, to worlds not on my little map.

They went in droves. The depredation such
as left no choice, English-Made-Easy in
their pockets, and the rough guide to getting rich.
Then travelled to and fro, like Thomas with Yeats;
O'Donoghue his 'rainmaker' at Colwyn;
on that fine line between nation and mental states.

MEDITATION IN A PRIVATE GARDEN

This is a companion piece for sure,
for here we toil and share our labour
like the original pair, no moping or lusting
after lost youth, but what adds up
to agape's absorption from the world.

If the snake oil salesman should call
we'll not hear him out here, no matter
our plot's so small, we can hardly
lose sight of each other even with
our backs turned, as we reach or kneel

to bud or bed, trimming and snipping
and digging, talking intermittently,
pragmatically, apropos of whatever it was
should go where, and the garden blesses us
with its classic thought and shade.

Virtuous purpose has great merit,
for it can banish desire for solitude
and yet provide escape from company...
Which is the better way to be? To ask
a question of a mystery? Or answer with one?

We work the soil here so diligently
anything might grow in its season. I say,
I can't decide in which mood I'm happier.
You think I prefer an edge of satire,
some bittersweet version of pastoral?

I certainly like to prune the apple.
But best of all, I like the fall, slapstick,
as the first cold snap signals the game is up
and gravity grasps the nettle itself
to bring everything down to earth.

POEM

The day's rain swells the river,
the spate bigger by the hour.

What foils the salmon leaping
is not, as I thought, too much water

but too little. So let it pour and pour!
Then what's not faith is timing.

ARKWORK

On the Loss of 'The Princess Victoria', January 1953

'Abandon ship all you who enter here'

(i) *Noah's Flood*
The known world, and the unknown, under water,
and by the mid-point, as one might suppose,
where things had got to heaven knows.
And had the scuppers failed in that foul weather
or had we struck a hidden rock there was
no other ground on which to run aground.
Then all was lost and no redeeming lost-and-found,
no memorial, come whatever time to pass...

A single window like an eye, reeling,
three tiers or decks but none to promenade
and take the air on, or watch the evening
sun go down, with a drink in one hand,
the other on the taff-rail. No headway made,
though the world go round, no good dry land.

(ii) *No Doubt*
But tell me what the mystery's about?
The price we pay to keep ourselves afloat
exacted by a metaphor, no doubt.
A boat, I cry, your kingdom for a boat.
For it's not mine, and nothing is: the air
I sing and breathe all begged or borrowed
as were those dreams I thought I followed,
a stowaway who can't afford the fare.

You know those times when you would rather not?
The weather's up and blusters at the door,
the rain is down your neck and in your boot:
on such a day did Noah's flood begin
but still you sail as if ordained by law.
Well, such a plight it is that I am in.

(iii)
No good? No good? If land, not to be seen.
Kirk's on the hill but the hill's drowned
as the river rises up and round
and like Leviathan lays waste the scene.
Kirk itself's an ark on an uneven keel
but nothing of that old salvation ever
freed itself from violence: O brother,
for whom was hellfire and it was real.
Hell to pay for her owners none the less.

A nineteenth-century disaster in
the twentieth, his honour said. A slight breeze
in cat's paws crossed to the Causeway
as he spoke. The sea waltzed in and out again,
as it has always done, since Noah's day.

(iv)
Two hours out on the interminable
waterways, he signalled she was no longer
'under command'. The wind blew stronger.
The sea rose and his ark unstable
rolled round the rolling world. Still nothing
in the offing told him where they were.
Pure storm, pure element of air
and water beaten to the eye, drowning.

Any port in a storm he bade the raven.
Anywhere, he said, from Ararat to Osney,
not knowing how near she stood to haven
at the mouth of Belfast Lough. (God save us!)
But the day proved just one more - of how many? -
in the wilderness of hope and loss.

(v) *In memory of David Broadfoot, Radio Officer*
O steadfast Captain Ferguson what doom
your ark, what fatal ferryman you proved...
Souls perish and hands go down. She waved
him off as usual, from the front bedroom,
and the house as empty as a widow
in the buffeting wintry shock of day.
This woman mother now so far away
of my wife's cousin's husband? Somehow
related, anyway... and how remote
that morning (many tumultuous lines

cross-hatch, scribble, lower the boat),
as David Broadfoot gave his life,
sinking fast… radioing lifelines
to the last, and, choking, came to grief.

(vi) *May-Day*
A single window like an eye and morse
remorselessly…remorseful. Always when
the drama is in progress, another one
is going on behind the scenes, and worse
remembrance runs and runs like the mousetrap,
a play within and another one beyond.
So that was Rosencrantz, packet to hand,
and Guildenstern, blithely taking a nap.

Had they the serum to hand in Eden
would any of this have fallen out?
Noah went to the bridge: Leviathan
wrapped him round and round his heart,
saying: 'It's all in the telling, whether heaven
or hell, and all in the name of art.'

(vii) *Altogether Elsewhere*
They went aboard in ones and twos,
in no great shape or order. The usual
kind of crowd and would be casual
but for those quayside feeling queasy blues.
They were thrown together… (Excuse me.)
But they'd need more than dry Ulster humour
to keep their spirits above water,
as they gasped and struggled in the sea.

Meanwhile, deep inland, the steading hove to.
As if a poem on the shipping forecast
was that moment conceiving. The radio
announced the disaster, in patrician English:
the old assault and innocence lost
that poetry is heir to, and the Irish.

(viii) *A Cowshed High Up in the Alps*
    'In the mountains, there you feel free.'
    T.S. Eliot

Is it really that we want to be free
of memory's dirty tricks? Without which
there's no idealism, no utopia, and not much
else to speak of; and the cowshed you see
high up in the Alps, an upended ark,
is a cowshed. But if we could strip it
of association what might it not
be said to be? Shelter, hafod, womb-dark?
None of the above. That way madness lies.
So Gudrun can only stand and watch
as Gerald wanders off into the snow and dies.
I lived in an ark once, all run aground
upon the rocks. I can see it from here, which
believe me is the better way round.

(ix) *Noah: The Complete Works*
He might have landed on Mont Blanc.
He might have grounded on Parnassus.
He might have drifted by Ben Nevis.
He might have struck a rock and sunk.
He might have voyaged up the Congo.
He might have cruised above the Nile.
He might yet round the Horn in style...

He might have travelled incognito
and told another kind of shipwreck tale.
He might have written Robinson Crusoe
or the one about the great white whale.
He might have shot the poor albatross
like cock robin with his bow and arrow…
And had he not how could we count the loss?

(x) *Art Lubber*
Keep your feet on the ground that's how.
Those 133 lives lost know no accounting or
grieving now. Just nine poems out before
she sprang a leak below the bow,
as if she'd struck the Whillans of Larne.
Like young Morrison all out of luck,
he foundered on a heartfelt rock
and could neither sail on nor return.

Cut your losses and swim for it. Think of it
in metres and work to improve your style,
and do what you will with the lifeboat it
can be to no avail, either to the dead
or the living, if you haven't learnt to sail,
in the name of art, as the monster said.

(xi) *Covenant*
In my heart's wake a catalogue of wrecks,
drownings: from Deutschland to Eurydice,
from 'Lycidas' to the 'Cast-Away', the
Mariner's guilt, the spectral decks,
a slave-ship hulk, old Ahab's curse…
creation myths; survival stories
recounted by Ulysses in extremis.
The sea has many voices. And nothing worse

happens but happens there, unless in verse?
Ten sheets to the wind and half seas over
and I could to my own self be true (what else?),
I'd go down again with the good ship Elegy
on a dog-toothed covenant wing-and-prayer
to see all the world as it flashed before me.

NORTH CLUTAG

(i) A POACHER'S HANDBOOK
My undercover name
north-northwest indeed
of where I make my home
down here among the dead.

I was found in a dark wood:
last light, running at its edge
(filigree, wood-cut), stood
caught in a thorny hedge.

The page beneath my hand,
now foxed, gave all it had to give.
But my heart was green and
wanted what it couldn't have.

Light and air, North by your leave...
Sprigged lettering hedged about
with too much to grieve
for and too much to leave out.

(ii) CLUTARCHE (1594/7 spelling)
Don't look back? What else to do?
Having put your hand to the poem
fit yourself for the kingdom of earth.

And as you reap, so shall you sow.
You have no say in any scheme.
Do what you will to keep the faith.

(iii) ANDY WALKER (PLOUGHMAN)
Not him but his father
who went for a soldier

and disappeared: lost in the action
of that wild fiction.

One of the fallen unsung
resurrected in his son

who followed the plough again
as this one follows the pen.

(iv) i.m. MARGARET WILLSON (d. 1685, aged 18)
A stone cut with 'a waved top'
shows how the waters rose up.
They buried the martyrs there,
on Wigtown hill, above the river
where they drowned, and never
a dry eye in the house. And never
would Margaret 'hear' or 'swear'
but kept her covenant forever,
as the sea rose again, like Christ
Himself, but with a salty taste,
until the drowning light was past

and all the world in brutal haste
went about its business to the last.

(v) COVENANT
Whenever came a time to raise a glass
and toast: 'God save the King!'
he'd say beneath his breath, for all to hear:

'If He pleases... if He pleases...'
As if he was John Knox, not merely
your parish blacksmith John McNeillie.

(vi) THE CARRY (Pronounced 'Kerry')
There were days he said it changed
several times an hour, the skies confused.

Whether as night fell, or in the morning,
and what might come, come without warning.

Fair days or foul, a good practical Scot
he proved, and master of his craft.

At furnace and anvil forged shoe or share
or tinkered some ingenious repair

to keep the harvest running, one step ahead
of the weather, in whose cup he read.

Fay as they come, fay as any spalpín Irishman,
or foolish poet, with all his loss to scan.

(vii) FOR GREAT-GRANNY ELIZABETH (*née* MCGARVA)
Here I am then at your door,
late windfall of life's storm.

A man who'll tinker at a poem
until the kye come home.

For 'a wee bit hot water'
Mistress if you please.

SLOWER

Slower, the sign said, gently, inviting reflection,
expressing welcome, down the single-track way
through the grove, not an injunction. So we wove,
slower, through the rain, headlights strobing where
blonde sponge-like Charolais gazed at us, balefully,
drenched together under an oak. Only in Ireland
somebody said, too readily. But slower, the word itself
weighed in me all week, an undertow to all we did
and all we saw and heard during our stay,
on the banks of the Swilly at Castle Grove. Derry
just down the road, and farther east 'the real loo-loos',
as a guest from Wicklow said, up to no good.

Slower, the day called, rooks funnelling up through
pristine aftermath and down to dewy meadows where
the river slithered out over itself. Mrs Sweeney, a name
to conjure with, told us the history of the house. How
when the line of Groves died out, a niece of Queen
Elizabeth acquired it, but when Lord Mountbatten
got blown up she opted out. (Sotheby valued the contents
at over a million.) So the dairy-farming Sweeneys

seized the hour and moved in; and slower they thought,
slower they said, naming the rooms after Irish writers:
Swift, Wilde, Joyce, Yeats… as if to inspire
a happy addition to the literature of the Irish hotel.

Slower, they all said, but one told me how the Irish Army
had haunted his fields after Bloody Sunday and
the talk was of invasion, to liberate occupied territory
from the bloody Brits. Another said the 'Bs' hadn't
been all bad. You knew where you were with them.
But talk as they might, in sixty-eight no one saw it coming.
He'd been sent as a boy to school in Derry and when
the women of the Bogside chased the peelers out
with broom-handles, the boys thought it a great joke.
And so together we juggled terms and jinked down
unmarked borders of speech, like smugglers, refusing
to pay duty on our goodwill, shadowed by Good Friday.

Slower, history beckoned, sifting its river-silts so
late in the day, yet in the long run, as the man said,
in the long run we are all dead. And one said you know
if they had a referendum in England it would be for
a United Ireland. They want this over. But slower
our eyes said, slower, as we wearied of our troubles
and went upstairs to bed. Slower, we sank down,
out of our depth and beyond help, returned to our
failings and powerless privacies, our commonplace
desires: the bride and groom flown, and the wedding
of two worlds behind us. Maybe in their lifetime? Or
slower yet, their children's? Or their children's?

from PART I: SONG IN WINTER

WINTER SONG

(i) CHANSON D'HIVER

I lie awake for more than half the night,
like a northern summer, my mind suffused
with light, though it's deep winter still
and long days are a dream that's yet to come
when short nights keep a bonfire never quite
gone out. I call this hope, if you will.

An oyster-catcher on a roof-ridge pipes
night ashore and day aboard in light
like wreaths of smoke; and, even from this far,
I can hear the tide crunch packed air,
quarrying the bay for white sand.
What is it that I cannot say, to you?

It's not that I dislike the cold air:
rain turned to sleet and flakes no longer hesitant
blinding the headland with light,
like a poke in the eye with a sprung twig,
and metaphor stranded for the duration
out in the wilderness of frozen pipes.

The world as it is I can take if it exists,
as appearances, and commonsense, insist.
But they always insist too much, the facts
and certainties their own undoing,

for life is all becoming, and this winter night
I lie here wide awake because of you.

(ii) ROAD CLOSED

This morning in January jumps
at the woodside, and the world rocks
as if hungry for the vernal equinox.
Headlong we go. Nothing damps
our appetite for change. Time ticks
too slow. Who can abide it
hanging so? What once was valid
is no longer. Who doesn't know?

Sheared branches fly, and ivied limbs
break under the weight of air,
blocking the road. Pensive or vacant, we queue,
out of sight, and into mind. The view
explodes and tugs, as at heart strings.
And beyond our fish-tank staring-out
it hurls ahead, reckless of destiny.
As, just to think of you, my heart hurls me.

(iii) WINTER

Winter has nothing to offer but itself.
It is the year's last resort, though holly
come into berry and mistletoe offer relief
to deciduous life and the ancient sky.
Winter will do for me, the thing itself.

(iv) THE SHADOW OF A BLACKBIRD

It wasn't snowing and it wasn't going to snow.
Snow had become a thing I used to know,
a metaphor whited out of every latitude I knew.
So when it crossed my mind, I thought of you.

So winter might have looked to its laurels,
no longer variegated, no longer what it was.
And the blackbird stranded in its branches
looked the shadow of a blackbird too.

(v) O WOOD!

This wood-and-leafmeal air,
dank and frosted, deadens
and scours the earth, as if
for signs of life. They're
somewhere, I tell myself,
wired to the weather.

Disturb my heart? I am already
wrecked beyond belief,
whichever direction you turn me.
O wood! would I were ever
as certain of rebirth
from such wreckage, as you are.

Those who would put
a Stoic face on it, I number
well, their wood for trees.
I'm of their timber,
but I know their belief
isn't all that it appears.

(vi) FEBRUARY SONG

It was a false evening
very like a dawn.
I heard a song-thrush singing
from an empty thorn.

Something in the light
encouraged it to sing
and as it sang so I have sung
and been as wrong.

(vii) LES FEUILLES D'AUTOMNE

Autumn leaves, packs its bags,
and winter inherits empty trees.
Metaphor as symbol begs
to embark again on violent seas.

What put the no in November
won't be gainsaid.
No more I, though I remember
mal de mer and wishing to be dead.

No more I, whatever that might mean,
before the sea's ego.
Everything and its season
gone before you know.

(viii) UNEVEN SONG

Winter trims the gas under the Michaelmas daisies
and purple turns to ash.

Once ripe with promise, October fails
and sinks into November's darkness.

I knew you in my guilty innocence
when autumn was no corruption.

Then even winter fell to earth to rise again
in frosted brilliance.

The prototype of spring and resurrection
promised like seed-time in its first green season.

But, in inverse proportion now, eavesdropping
on an Oxford evensong

and prayers of repentance,
I step into the dark content to be brought to nothing.

(ix) TIDINGS

In the long nights I began
as if setting out for spring.

Making preparations for the bride.
Laying all bare.

I lingered bitterly through Easter,
then gave up the ghost, on the weather's cross.

What might have been cannot be written off,
as being without meaning.

I'd lived for something more
but will make do with loss.

(x) SPINNEY

These are long days now,
though winter days are short,
prey to frost, and even snow,
or uneven, migrant north,
rare as winter lightning
used to be, chasing death.

Like a blood-clot in the thinning light,
thickening up, vestige after-glow,
with angioplastic blackbird
scolding through, memory
false and true, to free the heart
from where it cannot go.

BOOZY WEATHER

What I think I'm doing here, killing time,
in this London hotel bar, I do not know,
the evening bustling in early May,
the streets thronged with passers-by.
Too early, surely, to talk of winter?
But brooding as I sip Grey Goose vodka
I glimpse a skein of wild geese as they cross
a wintry sky… On which high octane
lost trajectory, I find myself, and leave

the world behind, back in my comfort zone
of cloudy weather, where possession is
all tenths of the law, and I am dispossessed
of here and now, and all my little grief,
for half an hour or so, seems what it is,
mere *comme il faut, encore une fois...*
and not why is the world the way it is?
But these others, in their happy hour,
laugh, as if they'd laugh for ever,
passing their drinks through the air, to one another...
in the press at the bar. Boozy weather
it is for them and the heart in chaos
weighs anchor for the evening's crossing
to a happier oblivion than any seems
possible to me, for my sins, in which
I don't believe, and sorrows, which I do.

GRIEF

If forgetting were an option
what would you choose to purge?
Did anyone ever put such a question,
the offer you can only refuse?

Here, now, where evening thickens
into night, I cling to light
at its diurnal death. Brackens
feather the headland. I forget

how often... But I forget nothing
about you, and remember as if
you were everything
though now that everything is grief.

HOW DEEP IS THE OCEAN?

It is my sixty-first year to my doom:
I am at sea and more or less alone.
There is a place I commonly call home.
There are some folk I love to call my own.
I know some fragments of a heartfelt song
that tells how every day man lives and dies.
There is a broken net I trawl along,
a leaking haul of fishy memories.

I have a code I tap when things go wrong
as fog rolls in or waves climb out of sight.
I know the mirage and the siren song
but still the dream farewell, at setting out,
allures, and back-ashore's look-bright.
As if I know what death is all about.

HIGH AND DRY

This vessel is unreal, forget
the starry archipelago.
Those haulers... how
they bore her up through
the dune, I don't know.

So I bear this, and turn it,
roof-up, to keep a secret,
safe from winter, aware
some of us won't see spring
together, whoever we are.

Time's here by the sand-grain,
in abundant galaxies,
an excess of it, like memory
paint-stripped, on a salt wind,
bringing tears to the eyes.

LES POÈTES MAUDITS

Between salon and saloon: a porthole,
in a *paquebot*, a late moon passing over,
making its crossing between
l'art pour l'art et mal de mer
and no one to talk to but oneself
reading the cursed poets in parallel text.

The nib of the ship pauses in mid-air,
then plunges on, into the inky morning.
All reality's a journey. All coasts
are fictions and all harbours symbols.
Cursed and blessed we go
to see what we believe, good hypocrites.

I.M. JULIETTE DROUET

Of all of them I would have preferred you:
like those backing girls in Motown
I adored in youth, or Mary Magdalene
(forgive me, please...) and still do:
heroic girls with walk-on doo-wop roles,
victorious victims of the powers that be:
dream-women who make it through
to *papier maché* dignity, as flesh fails.

I want to spend the night with you,
soirée à deux; you in all your finery,
shabby-genteel, glitter of old jewellery,
remembrance found in your lost gaze,
and you will tell it like it was
to strut your stuff, and play the muse.

LOVE IN THE LANGUAGE ROOM

A room three storeys up
and many a story round
where ungainly albatrosses we
tried to leave the ground
as if speaking in tongues
dans le nord du pays de Galles.

Sexe et tristesse
à côté de la mer,
là-bas-longing to be elsewhere,
aground on Dogger Bank.
Not everything's translation
or there'd be no originals.

In the spirit is the letter.
So I come to you,
my heart laid bare and
dictionary in hand
with my story in my native tongue
for you not quite to understand.

LE RÊVE

i.m. Villiers de l'Isle D'Adam et Pauvre Lelian

Must be lived in to be lived out –
stepping from Le Gard du Nord –
whatever its gender, however
housed, or homeless, under no roof
but the sky, above your misspelt heart.
How many of them came this way?

Arrival is also departure.
I am fluent in that grammar,
I should say, before you start
to put me right. Fluent, I say,
le mot juste, where otherwise
no justice saw the light of day.

SOLO IN NEW YORK

The pianist-singer plays and sings
'I'm beginning to see the light'
though night has fallen, dark brings
reflection to glass and to the heart,
aided by Scotch on the rocks.

Always that beginning charms me
and not 'I can't get started...' now,
as the rhythm section kicks
inside my head and I begin to blow
my solo here, my ballad elegy.

A brief riff above Park Avenue,
'Solitude' my bride, thinking
as I write of no one else but you
as one who's seen the light
and cannot help but sing.

SUMMER READING

Upheaval of the heart, turmoil
like revolution brought to grief.
Then second empire censorship,
a new regime, an exiled life...

Haunted and shadowed
exquisitely all summer.
What has Nostromo to do with it
but a lighter of silver to launder?

MISLAID

I found it in the new grass
a song-thrush egg and pricked it
with a haw thorn
and blew it out as I'd not done
in nearer fifty fitful years'
remembering.

Then the orange yolk still
tacky on my fingers,
I fumbled for my notebook
and my pen
to prick at it again
where life had been.

SPRING CAMPAIGN

Spring has no business here this month,
or so you'd think, this damp cold morning,
as the brisk couples, ramblers with maps
hung round their necks, ornithologists,
pensioners with dogs, all come and go,
about their constitutionals at Blenheim as
a gunshot resounds the length of the Estate
and cold as a brass monkey the Duke
stands upright on his column.

On Woodstock Lake, two men fishing in a boat
keep warm by burning charcoal in a can.
Its smoke hangs on the air and drifts
as they drift, in a haze or trance,
as later glimpsed through trees, all gauze
before my eyes, and in the water. Briefly,
I imagine black-powder cloud and carnage,
courtesy of which I dream along
thinking of you, and of the spring.

Like titmice flitting in the crowns of trees
I go, with even less than Lilliput
to my credit, my purposes obscure
beyond mere exercise and habit,
pausing to scribble in a notebook
the premonition of this poem for you
withheld, as at this time, everything
in the day denies by glance and light
something, reveille, I think I'll call it,
that one dawn soon will fill the air.

THE RISING OF THE YEAR

The one you'll never hear again.
The one you'll never see.

But were you to get lucky
you wouldn't be mistaken.

There'd be no embarrassment
and no disappointment.

No short shrift as might be human
after so long but as if only

yesterday they left off calling
like the faithful ones they were

night and morning
at the rising of the year.

HEDGER

A true hedger hedges no bets,
bending and cutting, warp and weft,
thorn and ash, sycamore and hazel,
his barricade to all but light,
pour encourager les autres…
come spring's uprising of the heart.

GREAT LEVELLER

To migrate into versatility before
Mont Sainte-Victoire not Parnassus.
To be alert to altitude sickness
and to prefer *mal de mer.*

The mountainous sea the great leveller
but above all, beneath all,
to keep the watch, the vigil,
and your course, to tack, and weather.

INTERNAL EXILE

Visitations, hauntings, travel...
a journey North
overnighting in the Isle,
lodged at the Steampacket
on the harbour wall.
Better to arrive than travel
though arrival's mythical
and comes with baggage.

BOTANICAL GARDENS REVISITED

> *'I saw the Spring return, when I was dead...'*
> Wordsworth

A fine spring day. The morning shines.
Too much billing and cooing to doubt
the future of pigeons, or humanity,
in this sanctuary from an uneasy world,

even for my unquiet heart. Sap thrives.
Take those two settled by the fountain with a picnic...
as if to rub my nose in it, they stand,
link arms and, glass-to-lip, drink
to each other with their eyes, then
mouth-to-mouth what's his is hers.
... Russian-style, I think, or Polish. But
seeing they sense my staring sorrow,
I flinch, and look back at my book.

NIGHTJARS

I wavered like the hour itself, eyes giving way to ears
as owls and woodcock in a blur
flitted through shadows of thin air
but never a nightjar joined them.
I stayed there waiting, none the less,
still learning things about myself,
the same things as usual. When
from nowhere the air filled with nightjars
rising with a whipcrack, and churring
to their hearts' delight
jamming the airwaves, until I felt
lost there on the heath
among the Nissen footings and flooded pits
and ghosts of airmen.

ARCTIC TERNS

Just so, there are towns where
arctic terns nest in the square
and last light harbours keep
night and sleep at bay, as
I remember, and remember you.

How incongruous congruities
make for beauty, uniquely.
Ever to see you again might
elude me, other than in memory,
among the fishing towns of the heart.

ANNO DOMINE 2007

I watched a pair of thrushes build their nest
in a laurel in my garden.
Stealing out now and then
as they had stolen in
I checked their progress,
first in building, next
when five eggs in the hen bird
started brooding
and at evening rain or shine
her partner sang.
Stealthily I stepped across the lawn
like a thief to see and not be seen.
Strong recognition I felt
but what was I recognizing?
Remembrance, tenderness,
in this dark year of our lord?

SUMMER MIGRANT

Here, again? And no doubt
and no doubting the difference
between us. For habit in you
is truth. What you repeat
is beauty, to the senses.
But mine is deadly,
seeking solace, needy, and
dependent on such fleeting
appearances to forget.

THE BIG SNOW

Just when you've cracked it
and worked life out
and how your little luck makes sense
enough, you take a hit.

Think of it as shipping a wave
out of the blue,
never due or overdue.
Think of it as falling in love.

from PART II: AT SEA

'It is generally well known that out of the crews of whaling vessels… few ever return in the ships on board which they departed.' from *Cruise in a Whale Boat*, quoted in *Moby Dick* by Herman Melville

LIFE-LINE

Be sure that you've secured it at both ends.

THE VOYAGE

poem on Mandelshtam's birthday

Trust to the day and to your craft.
Send the old quayside caveat
'Weather Permitting' to hell...
Turn three times anti-clockwise
in your swivel-chair, or on your heel,
only the daïmon or the muse
controls the tides. 'Poetry's a mystery,'
so wrote the poet's widow
from the heart, knowing the worst,
having looked it in its steely eye.
This isn't one of Stalin's barges,
up to the eyeballs, stark-staring mad.
No matter the world is
staring at apocalypse.
Embark! Set sail...!
What though we may never meet again?

NIGHT-SNOW

wee song for Sydney Graham

The real poem never ends.
The blizzard beneath its last footprint
is where we search in its memory,
the blizzard that is also night
as fresh on your face as snow.

Night-snow the ultimate
a body must weather, body I say,
but I mean soul
out on the manhole sea
where the littoral-minded sail

beyond Cape Metaphor to be.
And Sydney Coastguard keeps his watch
ticking on course for Greenock,
with Alfred Wallis at the wheel
aboard the good wreck *Alba*.

For who but a blind one can't see
Scotland from Cornwall? –
every small hour of the year
with the heart in the right direction
and a glass to his eye.

from A NIGHT ON WHALSAY

I

It is one thing for the mail not to come
another for nothing to come in the mail.
I'm not talking about love but words,
reading matter, news from the wars,
the latest collection by a great poet.
Don't talk to me about inner resources.
I too have had the Atlantic at my door all night
and my hearth the only thing between me
and the bareforked cold. Even the stones need light
to fall on them, and wind and tide to rattle them,
so they're never for a moment the same.
Just so, it's mistaken to say nothing has stirred
except for rhetorical effect, to catch
the idea of a flitting shoreline bird.

2

On the stillest morning and human kind
nowhere to be seen, but as you see yourself
front down, or your shadow walking before you
travelling westward to the rim of the world
and not a breath to flap your coat-tails
on the heart's shingle shelf. Not a breath
but your own, a life for once of your choosing,
whatever its hardships and downsides
as you step out, the world stripped to
essentials of sea, sky, shoreline, and bird –
infinity's limits. So island life intensifies
and shoots its net in the belly of the whale
and day and night you make your haul
come in and grow like so many bright herring.

3

Many a night, not just this one, I spent with you,
long since you died. I hear your father
poses for van Gogh these days, his true last look
yet to be seen. He'd have needed nine lives anyway
to deliver the sorting office of your mind,
and we're still waiting, parting the net curtain
for sight of the *paquebot* coming at last
leaping like a salmon, a mile high off West Linga
or far-flung Tory Island in a storm by Dixon.
Not archipelagos but arpeggios the *mot juste*:
spirit and letter one and the same,
in true haecceity. Live in the mind
the life that lives the dream
and leave the ground, for the ground of being.

4

Without which where'd we be? Too much at home.
It is one thing to call and find a person out,
another to visit without calling. They say
the dull-at-heart, you never spent a night in any sea-cave.
Truer to say you hardly put your head down anywhere else,
unless on a hillside to interrogate the thistle.
As if art and truth could be literal-minded
except by design and history's what happened.
It's not all in utterance or we'd be too overcome
to speak, but it is only in utterance
that things can be known and only in art remain
irreducible, open as the gates of a bird,
or the bottle I set down on midnight's kitchen table
to speak this, in mortal memory.

5

Of wilderness and keeping watch. Prophets
without honour in their country.
Taller seas than those beyond your window.
Ever more perfect storms. The thing itself,
in all life's brevity held at bay, where at last
the mailboat hoves in view, floating and soaring,
to deliver word of the world, manna heaven-sent
at your wind-battered door.
Its departure a rehearsal to delay thought
as once again it makes its exit, here through
a curtain of blown rain white as snow.
So one day for the last time it will ferry you.
But you barely look up, scribbling in your bunk
at the mind's stony limits of value and meaning.

6

Elsewhere, appeased, extremes clash.
Perpendicular armies strut their grief,
beyond a southern sea. True North is here,
where the heart's stayed, with mosses, comforted
with lichen, north of the wall; and winter sunlight
thrives, as thrives the human spirit in its wood,
at Hallaig, or by the deciduous Atlantic
off tree-bare Inis Mór, at Catraeth, as you said:
the invisible war, also a war of words.
Whose are we? Whose were we? Under what names
must history steal its march at our expense?
March meaning also a wall, a border or boundary,
as with Spring in our step we take new hope,
perennially, indomitable, human cost.

7

Now the present is heritage and history and
holiday in its season knocks at the door
of Grieve House, to look at your absence, grieve not.
There's no going back and who'd want to?
Even poetry has no reverse gear, though it
circumnavigate the ground of its being forever.
Even science works only in hindsight
slower than the speed of light preoccupied
with nature and origin, in dead time.
So what are we here for in this hovel Winter,
this hopeful Spring, this *hafod* Summer,
this mist of Autumn but to hold forward,
with courage and to sing according to our gifts,
as if we could do otherwise by act of will.

8

In my book that's not a question, though
to some it might be. I cannot speak for you.
It's a rule of grammar for one thing and
democracy for another, but in ventriloquy like this
who can tell where the voices come from,
articulating what for whom? No island is an island
entire of itself. Depopulate, regenerate...
the tidal rhythm insinuates everywhere:
the ground bass, with those twirly bits of yours,
bead-proof grace notes in the great music.
Don't ask for whom the bell tolls: it's too obvious.
The small hours we call them, as if to steady our nerves,
but they're the biggest of all.
No wonder nature prefers we sleep the night away.

9

Nature would make short work of us all
but the muse is always one step ahead.
She keeps the bottle pouring and the ink
regardless of the hour and ordered life.
The nights I've spent subject to her charms
are few enough but still I've had my out-of-body moments
scribbling to the rhythm of her intellect
and passion, mooching round harbours
with her on my arm as if we were lovers
destined for each other. She tells me song is being
and life both genial and tragic; that poetry
begins with an inner fact of consciousness;
and urges me to outsail the storm,
make landfall leagues ahead of elegy.

10

How self-imposed poverty spells freedom.
How poetry and poverty are almost the same word!
And both constrain to set truth free.
How you knew that... the inner fact of being
that holds its value forever, like gold.
I treasure the memory of my time still
and it's not too late to invest in it again.
Late though it is and not a matter of style
but of being and necessity, not to sleep on one's watch,
but keep the vigil singing along in the dark,
beyond the comfort zone, against the build-up to
farewell. For it's six in the morning again
and already the first ferry of the day
has let go fore and aft to catch the tide.

NETTING THE SCOTTISH FISH

Not so many miles north of Cawdor
nor in the worst of tide or weather
the netsmen aboard their coble
and their fellows on the cairn,
study every fold and quibble
of light on water through July...

Never naming what they look to see,
they call a fish a fish, from superstition.
And today again the unnameable
remains ineffable, invisible
to all but the inward eye. A condition
with a long history here.

THE LILIES OF THE FIELD

This country is my barricade,
my doorway and my heart's hearth.
Yet accretion and erosion attend
everywhere, as we live and breathe:
the world is all coming and going.

But for half the night last night
I had the Plough jammed in my skylight,
and the earth stopped turning,
as if god said: hold your horses,
consider the lilies of the field.

O VOS OMNES (TO G.H.)

(i) *Baudelaire: 'Quelques caricaturistes français'*
Walking in the other place, the poet
turned and said to me, 'Daumier
kept me going.' My search engine
ran on apace and brought me *inter alia*
not, as I'd guessed, to an august salon
but stuff about redressing wrong, the cretin
man in all his folly. (Nearby grave men,
without gravamen, haunted the architecture.)

And I ran on, a dog at heel
(pauvre chien désorienté, sans but
et sans pensée), detaining him as best
I could with foolish chatter. Uphill
all the way? At times I wonder
what the point of life is. Tell me, poet?

(ii) *Homage to KD*
Why do I think of Germany here? Witness
and conscience fell from the same tree,
the grafted *Apfel*. He strode on before me
like a great bear foraging through stars.
I told him what KD said of Günter Grass:
'He lied to win the Nobel Prize...
It was the lie itself, and not its cause:
we could all and many have lived with that.'
His brother ripped apart *Deutschland über alles*
in the star-spangled style of Jimi Hendrix.
But for cello. How German is that?
'They should not have bombed Belgrade.'
To find ourselves in such a state...
we've seen the best of our times, I'm afraid.

(iii) *i.m. Donato di Niccolo Donatello*
  'The upright shall live through faithfulness.'
  Habakkuk

'I don't need anyone,' he said, severely.
Thank you, I thought, and raised my glass
to my lips, pausing for reflection. Why
for god's sake am I doing this?
I looked my Acheronian oyster in the eye
and slurped it down. Bits of gritty shell
yet might make in time a pearl.
You'd have needed an oysterman's knife
to open the silence now upon us. Life
in death, or death in life? You lie,
I thought, you lie, remembering the roll-
call from Donne to Gurney,
Rosenberg to Rose. You need the dead.
'... The Habakkuk blew me away,' as he said.

(iv) *i.m. Sion Hill*
Nothing between us and the Urals? Nothing?
Cast your mind back. What memories are these?
Nowhere this side of Siberia bleaker skies
than I remember fieldfare and redwing
starveling darkened in winter's cold war.
Box-like de Havilland and Meteor
screeched across, ready for the worst.
Soldiers wolf-whistled my mother from a lorry.
Men touched their caps. Manners oppressed.
Hard to know what we think we mean by peace.
Never say worst, there is none? No less sage,
never say best? There was no golden age.
Yet in-between, no small part of the story,
how break of day can still seem blessed...

(v) *End of the line...*
I'd be wary of pastiche, if I were you,
I said to myself, wondering. But he phoned
that night and urged me on, praising a new
technical advance, regarding enjambement.
Heavy losses sustained to peace of mind.
The lift-shaft of self-doubt yawned.
Work as I might I could not go beyond
the end of any line, for even a moment.

For days I stared as if at years between
advances, the same as spoke volumes
of laboured silence in those times.
Don't go there, *comme on dit*, but play the clown?
I too am a very different poet from
the one I used to be, whatever iamb.

(vi) *Alms and the man*
Gurney and gunnery, too close for sanity.
Deep in darkness, he was himself once
on a gurney, electro-shock therapy
the morning's menu... Stunned into sense
not new to his experience. He was himself
once, or so he says – granted glimpses
of providential beauty, like Hopkins, his synapses
wired so. Google came up with nothing
like it in twice the time. He was himself
and after no one sang his song.
He never sought asylum from the world
but had it thrust upon him. Greatness
raved and after no one sang his song.
Alms and the man our sorrowful refrain.

(vii) *Bedside reading*
In Waterstone's stocking up on novels –
I mean detective fiction – poets don't
read novels, or write them, because they can't.
Name one? They're always something else.
Making ready for the long day's journey
into night, and no poem in the offing,
the game up, the Daïmon withholding.

I thought he might cease at any hour.
No tide-table. No return fare. No special
rates for parties travelling together.
No reservations, except those you'd call natural.
It's a short ride but while you can see
the wake of the ferryman, you've as long
as it takes to come and go there.

(viii) *Spleen et idéal*
The flotillas thronged, heavy as ever.
It was like Venice in high summer
but juddery in Dunkirk-black-and-white.
No leeway for casuistry... We sat
talking towards evensong. 'I hate,'
he said, 'the post '45 generation...
They betrayed literature, despising what they taught.'
Original sin the subject of his sermon.

Sins of emission thickened on the air.
We rode it out and railed against the shits,
leavening our fear with spleen.
'I wish I was dead,' he said. And Charon,
after Henry, made reply: 'My friend, you are...
As far as immortality permits.'

COMMEMORATION

And how far is it, the other journey? –
to resurrection day, the reception committee
in attendance at the pierhead,
reciting to the air in sure and certain immortality
verses on a newly unveiled plaque.

Here lies one whose name is writ in stone
who set sail decades back in cloudy weather
at the heart's funeral, some words
under a cloud, grief for a reckoning,
a balancing of books, the verdict open.

CNUT 2008

Leaning back, as if pulling at an oar,
his throne a-tilt, and his crown awry.

Never mention land-words at sea,
he recalls, an old superstition.

So his latest: never mention
sea-words ashore.

ASWIM

The sea furled and unfurled
on the flags, wave and rock.

Only look at it and it floods back,
the makings of this world.

The wall-maze another leviathan
and light falling as rain.

Cloud-wash. More stories than
you could shake a stick at

if you could find one
unless washed up ashore

sea-smooth, rubbed down
like Brendan in mid-winter.

IN THE MIDST OF LIFE

for Gail, in homage to Patrick Conneely

Or mist, I dreamt myself alive again, back from
the dead, beachcombing down that wintry shore,
lit by a sea-candle's orange-iodine flame –

the bay drawling, like a conch at my ear,
sea-spray and salt-wind whirling, and the dunes
whistling in a gooseflesh shiver of marram.

The day was like a night with no moon,
and the air crustacean, clawed; had there been a bell
it would have tolled, ask not for whom.

It isn't fanciful to think, heaven and hell
got married that morning, bride and groom,
and I there uninvited, one long-ago drowned

beyond space and time, in Blind Sound.
So seawards, singing my sea-words to the world,
flotsam-jetsam, heart's kindling, I strode –

with voices in my head, or not, I couldn't tell.
But both, the answer was, not either or.
'What a memory you have,' he said, and smiled.

He didn't know the half of it. Though he'd hand-hauled
in twenty fathoms the better part of his days
and seen such changes in a body's fortunes

would shake faith down to the rock of ages.
'Fish-stocks recover, left to their own devices…
It's never too late. But what can you do with the weather?'

The fog flurried our *mis-en-scène*. (Enter: a polar bear,
adrift on an ice-cube.) 'Curtains for us all!'
he cried, 'and they say we still have far to fall…'

Then he said, 'You know, I think those were *better* days'
and glanced as he spoke, weighing his words,
to the last syllable of what it is to know poverty.

Involuntarily, my mind flashed, like a night at sea,
aglitter with stars and villages ashore, barely lit,
and shipping lights, freighted with memory.

I struggled to agree but knew grace required it
and to be true to my heart, I said I feared it was so.
How can you live with so little fishing to look at

leaning on the sea-wall of old age? I don't know.
Winter indeed, the only tourist-free zone,
winter and its slender hold on light.

But you don't need to be old to be deranged, just
thin-partitioned from looking askance at life
and its short way with us all from the start. Mad

in the style of Father Ted, who now has his day,
his little immortality, when fancy-dress priests
and nuns invade the island, to party wildly.

It being our duty to laugh in the face of grief.
Yet to know which comes first and what it means
to name so many lost at sea and still believe in life.

And who knows what else might come to pass
to catch our leisure by the heels and wake us
from our sleep?... The sea was in and now the plane

roared on the runway at Cill Éinne, then took to the air
like a swan in reverse. As if to prove that
you can turn the clock back. And now 'Somewhere

beyond the sea...' the crooner croons
to Saturday night, singing so long ago...
Prize what's new, I say, but give me retro too.

'I know beyond a doubt...' he purrs... but
nothing will be as before, however many moons
go quartering the tides to make a haul of silver.

True places aren't down on any map, said Ishmael.
Thoughts run, beyond the page, and do not fit.
White is the colour of truth? So of the whale

that's never found on Ahab's map but in his head?
Never say never, nor either or? But both, I think,
inner and outer; and seize the hour's the trick.

For myself I was born in Thermidor. Unlike Patrick
Lobsterman, I'd sooner tire of life than lobster-meat.
But the sea is always greener, not to say the drink.

So with his sea-green hair Charles Baudelaire led
thought on a leash through the streets of Paris,
and sang so long ago, 'Somewhere beyond the sea…'

Là-bas… his bittersweet melody divine.
No matter the barman stands forever calling time.
Drink deep but keep your head above water.

As out here the islands keep theirs and prosper
while earth's luck lasts. Only the immortal poor,
and their poem, have footing that is surer.

However far into the hour you row dreaming
you'll wake from your senses. But waking may I
never hear you sing: 'Never again will I go sailing.'

Though now the curraghs are made of fibre glass,
and they have outboards… What is it in
habitude's reciprocity? 'No more canvas!'

Patrick laments. The quick pulse within,
inboard swell of ocean felt athwart,
dancing cheek to cheek, and sea to skin.

For intimacy's the best we have by heart.
Had I a hand for it I'd paint his portrait,
in oily impasto of sea-surge and cloud...

But this instead. Like poetry, fishing's an art, I said,
and when we put out to shoot a net
or spill a line, we do it with both thought

and craft, one stretched to the other, taut
but not too taut, as to be merely formal,
with give and take, between wave and boat.

As here and now, the soul's recital
turns on an oar, and comes full circle.
On holiday in Sardinia he bought sea-bream.

So once he caught them here, in autumn,
but never now, their stock fished out,
though time may yet shoal them back again.

He felt at home, islanded, and hearing 'Irish' in
the slap and splash of the Med, and loved at dawn
to see fresh fish landed, as for the first time.

Just what the thing itself must be about
when the scales fall from your eyes and you see
your life flash by. Then out goes the light...

What might be *better* days? Don't get me started.
True and untrue to say they lie ahead
as in the first line of a poem poised to be written.

But to say at once farewell, fare forward, and
haste back won't do. For all is nothing new.
I folded the money and put it in his hand

and thanked him for his company. He shook his rein
and the pony 'Grace' struck out for home, hoofbeat
for heartbeat… remembered all the way again

that tattoo round the bay, and down the strand,
where beachcombing for metaphor I meet
that one with a torch still burning in his hand.

I.M.LAH

There is no darker hour and you've fled North,
I like to think, haunting where I'd love to stay.
But my train speeds south, in the wake of storm.
So in the wake of you, my heart careers
to think how in the midst of death, I am in life,
witness to your obsequies, come Wednesday.
No one can stay and leave. But as you know
it works the other way. The image in the jimmy-mirror,
with just a wipe of the hanky stays
eye-bright for eternity… Just so your poems run,
like the river at my window, and can't be late, or early,
however fast or slow they make their journey.
But always and forever now, they go, and stay,
strong in themselves, as you were at leave-taking…

And would you put that one in your drawer?
Then pluck it out for print, months later,
to surprise me when a column fallen short,
at the hour's last ditch, needs filling at its foot
with an inch or two – pitched against purity,
sprung from the fount of our shared grief?
… Choose life? O *Flying Scotsman*!
The lesson of poem-spotting jumps all points
and *caesurae* like the purest drug or drink
ever distilled to the page. What else? Please ask
when next you see them: Dunbar and Burns,
Hogg, Scott… MacLean and Hay, MacDiarmid…
what other route you might have taken
out of this earthly station and still been here in time?

SEAWORTHY

What would change the way we think?
Not much, and too much to ask.

No good to say, step back from the brink,
but plough into the dark.

Even the best craft takes a lifetime
to turn round, into seaworthiness.

And on the way, many a drowned rhyme,
and many an SOS.

from LOSERS KEEPERS (2011)

LOSERS KEEPERS

Guardians of hardship's dignity,
all who stay on, and all who leave.
Send money home as you can.
And keep the heart's hearth alight,
smoored ash and midnight prayer
in the land of album and archive,
genealogy and all that's in a name.
For those of us whose memories
are not like these, whose sorrows
lost their footing long ago,
who never did belong except in this.

IN THE WILDERNESS

Who was I in the stranger's guise
and who were they in theirs?
I went among them, the latest of my kind,
while they were first forever to my mind.
And life itself so passing strange
that I had time for nothing else
and time I had as never since.
All spent to show what neither could
know or guess would come to pass,
word for word, the test of time.

A PORTRAIT OF THE AUTHOR

He landed and stowed his notebook
and heavy reading. It was winter.
Time of short days and long nights
with a swell on them all their own.

By day the draft under the door
and a deep window's long skies
turned his head from print to thought
and what precedes them both.

LOSINGS

These findings brought home,
objects of no use, unless to hold
a page against a draft or decorate
a sill or hearth, give weight,
featherweight even to weightlessness.
I should call them losings
even as they take hold on routine.

As if heard but not seen,
their presences in what proportion
absences? Tap the barometer
to know, from one day to another.
The heart's variable weather
begins with such things
once living, and unseen.

ARAN KEENING

i.m. Tom Hernon d. 17 November 2009 aet 87

My friend sent me a photo of his coffin
lying in state at Onacht, with his cap on.
... People from 'the islands' and
two sisters from America, the whole island,
came to pay their last respects.
I should have joined them, sent regrets?
But they barely waited and he was in
the airy ground, the moment gone.
I can see them though, in that wake of rain
and sudden break and gash of sun,
opened to order, over the graveyard,
and the 'huge' crowd of mourners gathered,
above the bay at Cill Mhuirbhigh where
the hero of my hour lived and died.
I was two weeks in at this anniversary,
my forty-first, a Tuesday to the day
he breathed his last: a 'dole-day', for irony.
His only holiday, his mother said.

THE LIVELY LADY

lost with all hands 1 March 1982

It's a downhill struggle, in an ocean of losses,
a shoreline of cobble and pebble and the sea's
hearthstone, swept after the tide-blaze, and spark
of wader-flight, starlight in the quick dark,
their calling like my own. Nothing changes?
That bay of 'silver sand' and marram, its embrace,

its waiting. I could settle for it were I able
to sail into view and put in there a while
for the boys to get a meal just up the hill.

DYING TO ARRIVE

I can see the months in my mind's eye
turning on the sun's wheel. Sense May
round the corner and hear the drystone
wind-harp wuther to the cuckoo's call
retuning my memory, returning me to the island
in late spring, the evenings lengthening.
My thought's starving for it now like a fish
chasing a feather on a lean hook.
It's less than a month away, I need no
reminding. I have minding enough.

LISTENING TO A FIDDLE AND REMEMBERING THE
ARD AENGUS

Air would be too coarse to describe it.
The faintest last pulse of storm lost to all
but the shade of memory, lingering between fiddle and bow,
like word of mouth, except I put it on paper.

One thing evades knowing. Two demand it.
So I see her driven 'swiftly' to destruction on the rocks
though to speak strictly Glassin was never visible
from the window of MacDonough's bar.

ENIGMA VARIATIONS

Let him press his fare into your hand
as discreetly as he likes, as if
to spare you your blushes and not his.
There are more where he came from,
living and dying, and no two the same.
Remember to keep your cards close
and tell him what he wants to hear.
Stretch the truth from ear to ear,
but smile to yourself, in your eyes only.
And he'll not begin to guess the places
you've travelled in all his years away.

A PITY YOUTH DOES NOT LAST

The young are aboard the autumn tide,
bantering their *amours* and *amour-propre*
turbining their hearts' blind wake, wide-eyed
with fairweather *joie de vivre*
and a last look that knows more than they do.

LOST ASHORE

I put out and stayed out. All night
I combed the wastes of my guilt.
Others too I saw by their lights
clinging to hope but not a sight
of wreckage still less of Mikey
MacDonough or Brian O'Flaherty.

We'd been pair fishing when
you know how it does it began
to blow and so we took shelter
under Black Head, bad weather
but not the worst. It was Brian
wouldn't heed, and off they ran.

I've been at their wake ever since
lost to sleep beyond sense.
My only blessing that I didn't send
my son across to help my friend.
Or how ever could I endure
a single day ashore?

NOTE: Truth to say, *The Lively Lady* – the boat concerned – was
poorly designed, and had no bulkheads to partition shipped water.
She would have had some 3 tons of water aboard 'and all in the one
place'. So she struggled to right herself in a strong sea. 'We've taken
a big one,' were her skipper's last words (in Irish). Then the radio
went dead.

EVEN KEEL

When the time comes
and the sea's at your heart's door
may you dwell in the present
and nothing either side of her.

RIDER TO THE SEA

'A man who is not afraid
of the sea will be drowned…'
I am afraid of the sea
and I am only drowned
now and again.
And no trouble to identify me
any morning in the week.

BOARDING

I've been aboard with men whose life it is.
They gently mock me on a small swell
of mirth and my lame lubber's step
down the iron rungs to where they're waiting,
their eyes like the eyes of gulls, salt-sharp,
and their humour not lost in translation.
I take the joke at my expense and at once
the wind-direction changes, slightly,
though never will I enter their world.
Time to admit I cannot live long enough now.
Do as I might, I'm here at their indulgence,
the best I can do, keep out of the way,
an art I've studied before and never more
than on days like this, on watch here.

POEM

Push the boat out again
hop your wet leg in
scuttle like a crab

take up oars and grab
the bucking surf
as if for dear life
prow up-reared proud
a roof over your head.

But lose your stroke
and hurled back
wallow beam-end on
soaked to the skin
awash against the strand
in no-man's land
of pounding foam
weed and flotsam.

No time to say
worse things at sea
but stern to shore
and bow once more
your blind horizon
pitch at it again
without flailing
oars unfailing.

ERRATICS

If you can't carry it in your head
close the book, take thought for a walk.
It's waiting for you at the door.
Put your hand to something,
a touchstone like this granite one
'a visitor from Connemara'.
And wish you might be as visitant
belonging so in all that's here.

METHUSELAH

There's no half-way
to call your own
and yet by now
I must have passed mine.

Wait here will you
while I retrace my steps?
Or go on ahead and
I'll catch you up.

THE CONNAUGHT RANGER

This is 2010, no fond past, and the green
Connaught Ranger rots at the wall
with all her rust and luckless gear
who swam so well down every tide
and survived the sea's hunger
to wash up here and die of starvation.

MEMORIES OF TRISTAN CORBIÈRE ON INIS MÓR

Coming up from the shore, the sea moored up,
the day at its last horizon, a glimmer of lights in the villages
clustering in pale imitation of the constellations,
and flocking waders, out here where light pollution
still barely subsists and the breakers are all air
and sea-turbulence and fish-basket, marker buoy,
net-tangle, bleached spar – the *echt* jetsam
of a lifetime ago even now, I met Bernard le Floch,
a man I never thought to see again, newly blown in

from la côte d'Armor, a Breton man who knew me
then for what I was, I saw at once, but never thought
to ask just what that was. And too late now, for sure.
He knew so well he smiled to hear the way I talked
of poetry and Tristan Corbière, as I gave him a tour
of the sights: *les chevaux de frise*; the worm's hole
by the meadow of the horse; the cliffs I climbed
to fish… as if I had all life within my grasp.

TIGHT LINES

What fellowship in lies and well-met
the squeezebox space between two hands.

The weighing eye, the heart's net.
See how truth expands.

SEA-GREEN

The tide running brackish. Sea-green bass
gleam down memory's current into
the jostling river-mouth. Surge of shoal
school my soul as never to be rewritten,
scold of gull and pipe of wader skirling.
Come what may, wait for no one now, all
aboard for loss and gain, whatever the hour
day or night, tide-table pinned to the sleeve.
Do you remember? Piece it together,
the two-piece and the rest on the ribbed
instep-breaking barefoot frothing flood.
The world from stem to stern possessed.

GOOD-BYE

Don't tell me absence makes the heart grow fonder.
Tell me about presence.
So summer whispers to the wind's scythe.

WALLFLOWER

I never wanted to, but put me through it
I did, imagining my shyness to be
undecided, and sometimes finding pity.
But I look askance at them now and all that
marriage has entailed, for those forward
blooms who couldn't bear to be ignored.

RUIN

The Gaelic word ruin
translates as desires.
The eye wanders here
and the mind wonders
where these two meet
at each other's wake.

SAINT BLACKBIRD

In whose footsteps, I wonder,
the stone step worn to a hollow?
Stooping in and out
at the lintel, as I flit too.

Between light and dark, wet and dry,
or damp, coming and going.
Winter squalor and bitter cold,
light enough for a silhouette only.

Or midgy swarming summer
tasting of cut hay and dung.
They'd more faith than sense, I'd say,
to keep body and soul together.

HOMAGE TO HAY

*Seven songs in homage to George Campbell Hay
(Deòrsa Mac Iain Dheòrsa) 1915–84*

(i) *Seeking*
See her tugging
at her muse's mooring,
restless to be gone,
the live-long night
her day: eager
to put lines between her
and home, out at
the edge of death
to shoot her net.

(ii) *Notes on a Menu at Loch Fyne, Walton Street*
I used to wonder as a boy
how far out the tide could go.
Spring tides I mean
and now I know. So
spring-times on the hill
above the west shore still

run out forever too. As if our
lives had never been.

O smokehouse shade…
talking to that waiter
who never saw a fish in water
if that is you I see there
on the other side: tell me
'An e bradan a th'ann?'
Or a cock sparra? Tell me:
how goes the plash in heaven?

(iii) *Sleeping Rough*
I met one sleeping rough and gave him money.
'Thank you,' he said, 'for treating me like a person.'
'There but for the grace of god,' I said,
and meant it no more nor less
than he understood. 'Thank you,' I said,
'for treating me like a person.'

Though I'd bring all men low if I could,
if only night and morning, to see them
humbled in their vanity, cold and near to death,
that they might yet awaken, finally.
But while I can't, I'll give you what I have
to help a shade who's sleeping rough:

Far from your family and your people, missing
in Dublin or the Pentland Hills, dreaming of Tarbert…
The least of all your ills: that lodestone faith you had
and independent heart, that always 'meant it', sure as
the North Star and the muse's Stella Maris,
would steer you home again, from anywhere.

To your poet's calling, and the tragedy of youth: seeking,
and reaping, as the happy laughing boy did sow.
Were only the world beyond home a decent place to live
and die, for either Mochtàr or Dùgall, Arab or Scot,
and their like who know though Barra is far out,
yet it can be reached, if you mean it in your heart.

The art of haven-finding, one vowel short of the real thing,
but adequate for life on earth, at sea. So Ebbing Point
to Laggan Head might sing, flashing farewell as the fishers go
into the darkness. The way you went on your last disappearance.
You with the tongue of the people in your scholar's mouth,
for whom there was no greater truth to tell, no truer way to speak.

But too much, too true, for the worldly world to take…
That world too much for you to bear?
Although, between you and your life, whether in
grey asylum light, or fug of Poets' Kremlin,
you could always make poems that shine, like herring in
a ring-net: in the old language, in Scots, in French or even

the beurla, singing of suffering and the heart's Eden,
rolling in and out of boats, rolling on the wild ocean
in the mouth of the northerly gale. Your course set by
Arcturus and Arctophylax, keepers of Artos the Bear,
who show the way to steer and that
prayers of praise exceed those of petition.

(iv) *Dancing Days for Fishing*
But mine are not quite over
while I can keep
my head above water
and to the fisher's jig and reel
feel my heart leap.

Though snatching-hook
and tine of female joint
lie deep now in the dark
of my heart's bottom-drawer
and dream all night of the hazel.

(v) *Good Health to Christ's Body*
The other night as I stepped out
drunk down Merton Street I went
and heard drift on the star-cold air
the hearty droning of the pipes
and guessed it was yourself up there
a-passing round the drinks.

By Christ the hour danced about
and swam around my brain.
I cannot tell was it you or they
came first to mind that way
or did I wake or did I dream
from passing round the drinks?

(vi) *Six Oysters and a Dram for You*
Call him Calum Johnson if you want to
or Tom Hernon. We both saw what it meant:
a man might lead the rooted life, too late
for us to share it. I far later than you,
sailing into the four winds of my fate.
(However far short I fall… from you.)
As if that little boat was heaven-sent
beating its foot to the dance, as I said,
into a storm-force day in November
before I ever heard your name or read
a word you wrote, about the seaborne life
of the mind, and how it must body forth

in common faith, into the common world,
of common folk to be of any worth
to be itself that you might be your self,
battering home with a song, to Tarbert
or Kilronan. Though your 'Owain o' Sycharth's' was
the first land I saw, my native heath.
What though there's MacDougall too in me,
Munro, McGarva, as well as Mac an Fidlih?
What if like yours my father also wrote
a novel that turned a world on its head?
What though we never met till you were dead
and Michel Byrne playing helm's man
brought me again to 'Loch Fyne', to sip
oysters with my golden wine, and greet you,
your battered doorstop menu at my elbow?

How much longer will I live in England?
I don't know… if Oxford is England.
My sorrow is that I might die there
among the ancient shades, the ghosts of youth,
as if knowing no better: the life of wilderness
and durance of sea-scape, inch cape,
inscape, instressed to the very tidemark
of high hope, pitched against the weather;
faith to keep, in each other's courses,
each other's verses. O seeker reaper maker
singer of all we were set here to praise,
not true to any orders but our own,
and the lineaments of a shipshape craft.
How much longer, my dear one? For all time,
wherever death befall us, to survive.

(vii) *Reaping*
Have no fear, poor shade,
those men in white coats
are harmless ghosts,
fishmarket-men, lubbers
in the night's wild wake.

So what if you'd think
from the way they behave
you went to the rim
of the world for them,
for anything but the poem?

THE JOURNEY

I came back and stayed on
my head turned by a girl
and what I didn't know
about the place I was in.

Under the same streeling light
habitual to my mind, between
sea and mountain, I taught
myself another lesson.

How the familiar opens out.
How all horizons meet
under you, invisibly,
if you pause to think.

As prompted this morning
waiting at the quay for the visitors,
their cameras already busy
as they come ashore.

TAKING LEAVE

Delicate poems about shorebirds
or girls I'd put my pen to if I could.
But what do either need of me
immortal and mortal beauty?
Never too late for a young heart
to rule an old head.
But now I must pack and make tracks
to be ready for the ferry.

FIELD GUIDE

Here the information board tells us
what to expect to see, what birdlife etc,
and fact-checks signs of early settlement,
devotion and war. Go in ignorance I say
for the sake of it. Let what you don't know
work on you like prevailing weather.
Recollect emotion after the event,
consult the field guide at your leisure.

THE DEVIL'S ELBOW

I could show you where it used to be,
the left one anyway, where the road
home hairpinned in among the trees.
And winter and its wild night-weather
drowned the beat of Tammy's hooves
above the swollen Bladnoch.
What shade was there but yours,
what story but your own enacted there?

Unspoken because no need to say
when raising an elbow what was afoot
in that world still in living memory.

THE SHABBY BRAE

The wall that ends outside my door
began two centuries ago, more than a mile away
beyond the Shabby Brae, enclosing
the Earl's Estate, hard labour
for prisoners of war, Napoleonic officers,
children of *la grande peur* whose *chamois*
time heard as 'shabby', so they say.
The deer are here still. I can see one now,
a few yards from my window in the trees
emboldened by ten days of snow.
It seems to ask me what I make of it
and I don't know but return its gaze.

MILLDRIGGAN

A little goes a long way in no time.
In the blink of a boy's eye
a house, blue door, white lime
and the stream fleeting by,
painted and framed.
Nothing now you might identify
in the outside world
trusting merely to the eye.

THE BIG SNOW

for Finn McCreath

The old men would speak of it, with warmth,
remembering snow-buntings in the stackyard.
Miracles and snowflakes swarming hard
to hold their ground against wet earth.
How it caught even prudent souls off guard.
And what they meant by big was also lasting.
Men of '47. They could remember wartime news
of Russia as if yesterday; and being themselves still
horse-drawn, praised a shoe would spiel the brae,
of an icy morning, and I was one year old.
Now as old as they, or coming on, to play
their part I speak of rainy summers and
calendars turned inside out, deeper troubles
than ice or snow to guard against, until today.

January 2010

LATE SPRING

I wanted to put elegy into storage
as the album-game *de nos jours*.
So much loss. Not loss but longing.
I worked on the idea that presence
makes the heart grow fonder
but straightaway found myself here.
It was late spring, the days not yet long
stealing time down cold evenings.
And this to make good
something else I put no name to.

MILTON'S ITALIAN SONNETS TRANSLATED FOR *THE COMPLETE WORKS OF JOHN MILTON* VOL. III (OUP, 2012)

II

Lovely lady whose name honours beauty
Where the grasses by Reno grow green
And the noble ford crosses the Rubicon,
How destitute of merit must he be,
Who's immune to you, you who so sweetly
Gentleness and grace of spirit show,
And virtue's gift, shot from Love's bow,
And flower so loftily and nobly.
Whoever is unworthy of your love
Must guard the entrance to his eyes and ears,
Or else be granted grace from above.
For once your voice and joyous song he hears,
To which even tough Alpine trees prove
No match, but sway, so he'll succumb to love.

III

On a steep hill at evening, long shadows fall,
And twilight fails. A local shepherd girl
Waters a strange beautiful plant. It scarcely grows at all,
Parted from its native spring and soil.
So Love coaxes foreign speech from me, and all
I sing to you with nimble tongue is Babel
To my fellow countrymen. As by Love's will,
Charming Lady, proud and regal,
I swap Thames' beauty for that of Arno.
So Love willed and Love I know
Never willed in vain, as witness others' sorrow.
If only my hard breast and heart so slow
Were as good a soil in which to sow
God's seed and grow, as now you grow.

CANZONE

Young men and women ripe for love
Laugh and gather round to know:
'Why, why do you write about love
In a language you don't even know?
How dare you! Let us know,
So your hope won't be in vain
And your best wishes may
Be answered.' So they make fun of me,
Saying: 'Other streams and shores
Await you, green-banked waters
Where immortal fronds grow a guerdon for your hair.
Why burden your shoulders with care?'
I'll tell you, and you'll answer for me.
My Lady whose word is my heart says:
'This is the language of Love.'

IV

Diodati, I'll tell you something astonishing.
You know how stubbornly I've scorned love,
And mocked its snares, and how I've
Laughed? Well now the thing
Has impaled me: I'm brought low. Not
By golden tresses or rosy cheeks but
A foreign ideal beauty has my heart.
Her bearing proud and modest
With calm yet brilliant blackness burning in her eyes.
Her speech graced by several languages.
When she sings the moon labouring in the skies
Might go astray. Even if I stopped my ears
With wax, it wouldn't help, for from her eyes
There shoot such fires.

V

For sure, my Lady, your lovely gaze can
Only be the sun to me.
Your look strikes me so powerfully,
It's like the Libyan desert sun falling on one
Who makes his way across the sands there.
A hot vapour I've never known before
Burns in my side. A lover might call it a sigh.
It's new to me, pressing right through.
A pain part-hidden, confined and agitated,
Escapes a little, having shaken my heart,
And all around it's chilled or frozen cold.
The part of it that finds a place in my eyes
Makes every night a rainy night
Until Dawn returns, brimming with roses.

VI

Young, gentle, and artless as I am, my lady,
Since I'm unsure how to escape my heart,
I'll give it devoutly to you, a humble gift.
I've tested it often and found its loyalty
Fearless, constant, gracious, gentle, kindly.
When the great world roars and thunder claps
My heart arms itself with itself and keeps
Adamant, as safe against chance and envy,
And common people's fears and hopes,
As it is eager for distinction of mind,
The resounding lyre and the Muses.
My dear, I think you'll only find
Its armour less resilient where
Love has put its sting, that knows no cure.

from WINTER MOORINGS (2014)

WINTER MOORINGS

Anchored stern and bow, sea-logged to the gunwales:
So I have moored my mind for the winter ahead.
To be the more sea-worthy if all else fails
Come better weather and spring buries its dead.

BLOCK: A PULLEY USED IN RUNNING RIGGING

I cannot put it down
Or knock it into shape
That world and time
Inside my head
Once no less real than
Today and as ordinary
As daylight delayed in a rhyme.

I'm beached by the flood
Caulking my dreams
Haunted by such men
As Johnnie Rogof, Jackie Craven
And other names
No one remembers
Hauling nets in all weathers.

I think of them and the pulley
To their hopes
That drew them to sea
And the stars' rigging
Taut as ever aloft

About their obscure lives
In that Welsh estuary.

Sufficient unto the day their lesson
Their names signed nowhere
As if written in water
And no thought spared
But to immerse in that world
An example to all and no one
Hauling fish into oblivion.

STRONG LINES

Stars flicker to quick white heat and the tide
Glitters the shoals where waders pipe and scatter.
I shift in my sleep, as the waters break; and we ride
Towards youth and the mouth of September.

Sea-green again with fish in the estuary,
Their school passing through me into the Conwy.
I spend my days ashore making and mending
Memory into strong lines hooked on rhyming.

Too late to ask what that world means to me.
What could it say even if it knew my mind
By heart? We don't always see eye to eye.
There are more than enough losses to go round.

I cast my thought out as far as I can and wait.
The waters rush against me and I feel their weight.

I can sing you a song   about myself
tell of travels   toil and trouble
terrors on tossed waves   suffered at sea
(*you know I can   I've sung it before*)
night-watch nightmares   at the prow
crashing by cliffs   feet frozen
frost-bound   sea-weary
at hunger's door   soul-cares seething
hot round my heart.   The lucky lubber
has no idea   how I spent winter
(*from worst of November*)   in paths of exile
wretched and sorrowful   hung with icicles
hit by hail   on ice-cold sea
lost to the world.   Nothing but roar of icy waves
met my ears.   Only the swan's song
gannet, gull   and curlew cry
gave me pleasure   in adversity
not laughter   and drink at the bar.
Storms beat   wind-torn cliffs
icy-feathered   kittiwake called
dewy-feathered   the erne yelled.
No caring kin   can comfort the desolate heart.
Truly the burgher   merry with wine
flushed with pride   has no idea
what painful wandering   I must bide
and how often weary   endure
in the paths of the sea.   (*So I fare now*
aboard my glossary   battered by cruces
in ink-black night   chasing more than
imitation   more than word for word
de-Christianising   formulaic scribe-scribble.

No comfy reader   turning pages
knows what pains I take   and pangs suffer
at heart for her...)
                    ... Night-shadows darkened.
Snow fell from North   frost
gripped ground   hail hammered earth
coldest grain.   My heart-thoughts –
troubled   now I must venture
on high streams   of tumultuous brine –
urge me always   far from here
seeking homeland   of foreign folk.
No one on earth's   so proud of spirit
so generous of gifts   so bold in youth
brave-of-deed   dear to his love
he does not fear   what doom fate
might deal him at sea.   He has no time to think
of harp-throb   or receiving of rings
pleasure in woman   nor worldly things
or anything else   but waste of waters.
Who goes to sea   knows heart's care.
Groves blossom   burghs grow fair
meadows beautiful.   World quickens.
All things urge   spirit to embark
fare far   by flood-ways
though melancholy call   of summer's lord
the cuckoo bode   bitter heart-sorrow.
The lucky reader   blessed with comfort
does not know   suffering of those
who travel farthest   as far as they can go
in exile's ways.   So now my spirit flies
beyond my breast   over sea-flood
above whale-path   soars far and wide
to earth's four corners   – returning eager,

greedy for more   wildish destinies.[1]
The solitary flier's cry   urges irresistibly
the willing heart again   to take the whale-road.
And so for me   such heightened being
is hotter than   dead life on land.
I don't believe earth-wealth will   last forever.
Always without fail   one of three things
will render all uncertain   before the fatal hour:
disease or age   or sword-hate
rip life from those   doomed to die.
For every one praise   of the living is best
of children hereafter   for good deeds
against enmity   daring deeds
against evil …

[*manuscript damaged…*]

Days all gone   of magnificence on earth.
There are no kings   no Caesars now
no gold-givers   without dirty money.
Now fallen all   that noble company.
Joys gone. Weaker men   wield world-power
thrive through trouble.   Glory fled.
Earth's nobility   grows old and sere
as shall every one   the world over.
Hoary-haired   old age comes on
faces grow pale.   We mourn old friends
sons of princes   given up to earth.
Body can't avail   when life leaves.
Can't swallow sweetness   nor feel pain
nor move hand   nor think with mind. . .

---

1 'géosceaft ge-wild'. Among her numerous caveats, Gordon protests 'a
total want of authority' here.

[*Here sea broke aboard   lines chopped through*
kennings cracked.   He spoke his last word
on the walkie-talkie   down with both hands in the ink
unwished for fate   for even your enemy....]

NOTE: This version derives from the so-called 'Cill Mhuirbhigh Ms'
attributed to the Árainn Scribe (fl.968-69) by Giraldus Cambrensis
(?1146-?1220) who visited the island during his Irish travels. Giraldus
claimed to have discovered it 'caulking a coracle', among other Mss
whose thickness helped preserve it (BL Royal MS 13 B VIII (a)). Ida
Gordon dismissed the entire text as 'irredeemably corrupt'. Little is
known about the reputed scribe beyond a work on the age-old custom of
caoineadh and that he stood fiercely opposed to institutionalised religion.

QUAY

I wait at the quay
And the quay waits.
There's many a thing more lasting than a person
I hear it say
At no great length.

PILOT ME

Pilot me, I pray, evermore,
Adrift on the rock of the world
Chain paid out to rust's bitter end
And low-tide in time's estuary drained
To its dregs, on pause the moon's full O
Buoyed agape up above,

As youth keeps its counsel
And reels the world to its door.

Late now, leaning in the jamb, head full
Of tides on a conch-shell coast at my ear
Glimmering far-cry and groundswell
Heart foot-tapping at mooring
Waiting still as if I know what for:
Pilot me, I pray, evermore.

TROUVÉ: RIGG BAY

I come here combing the sea's waste.
Indigestibles from the whale's belly:
Weed rich as dung, plastic husk, and the rest.
No knowing what might catch my eye
Or how it might set me thinking on beauty.
What shape fate gives to objects –
The sea being fate and fate a mystery
Questioning all laws that cause effects
To trace anew old lines on the map.

Now I stumble on a purple fish box
That declares where it comes from:
FOYLE FISHERMEN'S CO-OP
Greencastle, Ireland (No Unauthorised Use)
By some slick wave thrown up
At dead of night on the rocks
A catch of thin air, brim-full
To lift away elsewhere my afternoon.
I've heard tell it's a long way to Donegal.

MACHARS: WAR & PEACE

i.m. Sam Rennie

Offshore beyond all tides, but those of time,
Wreckage of a Mulberry Harbour
Scars the bay at low water, a living memory
To just about no one now. Its warning buoy
Seems, from where I am, to tilt at peace
In waves so short they're almost calm.
The world on the other side waxes and wanes,
Now promising rain with prophetic clarity,
Now keeping its word in a leaden barrage.

'The Lancasters taking off from Baldoon
Had seven minutes to make it over Cairnsmore,'
An ancient mariner tells me; and I look
Towards the invisible hill to get the measure of it,
To hear their din in my mind's ear.
My grandfather, born here a blacksmith's son,
Managed a production line that made them.
But I keep it to myself, a secret
Like that underground factory in England.

       * * *

Set your self against the fullness of time.
Blind we go, and blind we see
What's new under the sun's brighter for rain.
Look anywhere and find beauty; landscape
-in-waiting, what you want it to be,
What you have brought with you to find:
Your heritage, unpreserved, lived day by day.

You have your own words for it
And need to hear them and share them.

Where steading names stand in for poetry
And resignation for happiness and sorrow,
The fortunes of dynasties as they rise and fall.
Now the old know only their own by sight,
The rest as strangers, native or in-comer,
As the future prevails like the incoming tide
Eager to erase and start again
In sure and certain hope of resurrection,
The circle unbroken by staying or leaving.

       * * *

The wreck submerges again and
A cormorant bobs to the surface
To see which way the wind blows.
An ill wind for one blows another good.
I attend to my post-cards. The tide falls.
By the time they arrive I'll be home
And living for the next trip here again
Knowing each time might be the last time
Either for me or for someone.

Casualty of life's storm, or casualty of war…
Like Sam Rennie, riddled with shrapnel
Fighting through Italy. Feel the pieces.
Watch them move beneath the skin
From Monte Cassino to Kirkinner round.
He's waiting on the other side for someone now.
And tell me about the peace here
And just reward for service to one's country
And how a soul might mend.

LAVER WEED

Once, he said, the local yield so poor,
They went to Achill Island via Rosslare
To harvest there instead. So far!
Only to find 'the sand was in'
And the weed no good.
But by morning the weed came clean.
Such a thing, it seemed a miracle of god.

A time and a place, I said.

Time was they'd drive from The Gower
North to Port Patrick near Stranraer
To work 'The Strand' and 'The Knock'.
The length and breadth of the coast,
Good shoreline folk still years before
Sent theirs by train, on trust to Swansea…
But time's not what it was any more.

Neither time nor place, I said.

LAFAN

Already your long low tide draws me down
And your *trompe l'oeil* of sailing through sand
Runs my loss against those mussel banks
At the mouth between island and mainland.

At mere memory of your name I drown
And all that sails in me looks to the lifeboat
Whether *Tillie, Annie, Isabella* or *Lilly* –
And *What-Ho!* herself and the Menai Light.

From the saintly life of the headland I
Take spare comfort, grateful for small mercy,
The life of the head and the brain-cell
Flashing intermittent signal blindly.

Blind as in faith, on the sea of language,
The eighth sea with its own ports of call,
A mirror world in the world's image.
Here I come again by Lafan to make landfall.

ISLAND HOPPING

Today, bleaker herringbone without break,
No herring either; the weave making its haul
Out of woollen clouds and thin air,
Metaphysical-material, and fine downfall,
Haunting the heart of what it is to be solitary
In company, not arpeggio but archipelago,
Whether at bow or astern
For the furrow's sake or the coulter
Into night's black house where the peats burn
Until the morning's morning, smoulder
Like memories remembered by no one.

BY FERRY, FOOT, AND FATE

a tour in the Hebrides

It's one o'clock in the afternoon.
The ferry unloads to load again.
Clang of ramps and chorus of ignitions,
Roaring juggernauts in pole positions,

Hiss of air-brakes, flash of lights, and hazard-
Bleep cacophony ushers us aboard.
Crewmen haul ropes hand over hand
As since time immemorial. Land
Floats and drifts off. Ahead six hours of sea
Siren some to *mal-de-mer* others into reverie
Dreaming according to their repertoires.
But wherever we go for our pleasures:
The bars or decks, the depths, the TV's
Comforts or those uplifting distant skies
Where evening distils a purer light
We'll all reach Barra before the night.

As for me, what do I bring in my bag?
Camcorder, notebook, an eye for a grey-lag…
Ash-stick in hand to beat off preconception.
No phone number for a mythical relation
Called MacNeill or anywhere but home
Where I now work at rhyme and half-rhyme
About an *arrière-pays*, an evermore,
Where sky and water wash ashore
And the symmetry of boats speaks of art
Within immensity, the sea: that keeps apart
While joining everything *arpeggio*
As here in the tattered archipelago.
For which please read a figure for my heart.
For which read too a figure for time's hurt
And every frayed and broken connection
Nothing can mend unless by invention.

The mind's near misses and far cries
Echo beyond time, and the seven seas.
All absence finds itself in presence first.
Departure heads towards now. Walk the worst

Out of yourself until you're rid of it,
Body and mind in step to a heartbeat.
I can't go on, I will go on, anti-clockwise
Round the island, east to west, the day's
Arc like a broken rainbow, yielding epiphanies
Sparely, as when I put to flight five geese
From a boggy field by the road and their
Beating wings hold me as if in mid-air
Yet firmly planted in the here-and-now
At something I would call peace although
The weather's din is deafening North Bay
And I have miles ahead at not half-way.
Which means I know my destination.
But how to make sense of devotion
To things-in-themselves of no certain end,
Neither as to meaning, nor peace of mind?
Unless to strip all thought of progress from
My progress and make space for a dream,
Or backlight to a stormy day, itself
At the same work, striking like lightning a shelf
Of rock where sea-birds splinter into flight
As once again I make it in by night,
Only this time somehow a different person
Dead on my feet but my mind wide open
In the wake of the day, still arriving, long after
Arrival at somewhere still yet farther
Off – neither ahead nor behind mean time
In a state of mind that works like a dram
That slowly turns the hour half-seas over
As glasses drown on the bar counter
And hands reach out in time to save them.

Broadband is down, they say. We tilt abeam,
Careening, cut off from the world…

Now Tigh na Mara's guests lie foetus-curled –
The elderly ladies, the two bikers, and I –
Make the night-crossing back towards day
Dreaming a silver-lining to the morning.
Dreaming of Mrs MacLean's black-pudding.
'The *making* of it,' she said, meaning the Full
Barra Breakfast I forego… or else I'll
Miss the 7am 'Lord of the Isles'
Who made it over in spite of gales.
Out of thin air materialised just now
In a smirr of rain beyond my window.
Now water becomes land and water everywhere
Becomes South Uist. As I step ashore
Fishing parties in four-by-fours (at least
Not plus-fours), leave the hotel and head west
Careless of the day's unfolding pastoral
That brings the crofters in to Lochboisdale
To sell and talk sheep (in Gaelic): ewe lambs
And gimmers and wedders, and rams
From Frobos and Rhughasinish;
And to down a drink before they finish
Talking of this and that… yon Dougie Walker
Missing three days, his face on a poster.
Identifying marks: a tattooed hinge
In the crook of each arm. 'Out on a binge…'
'Feared drowned…' So the present accumulates
Around Dougie Walker… and waits and waits.
I wait. There's more time to the hour here
Than you could shake a stick at and fewer
Miles. The clock flies out of the window where
Light and weather are the only measure
In the round of seasons. The tide's embrace
All there is to come and go by. The pace
Of things all dwelling and meander

As if in imitation of water.
I ride north, aboard the Post Office bus,
Via twenty-seven letter boxes
Wide-eyed-window-gazing, sole passenger
Of Morag Walker and her humour
At the work she has, her twenty-seven keys,
Her haul a small one on the best of days.
At Iochdar Junction, comes Archie Campbell
And the talk meanders as we travel
To another Northwest Frontier. 'Dreadful,
Dreadful place,' says Morag. 'That shithole,'
Urges Archie, whose sons have fought there,
One due another tour in October.
As is my son... We share a look and wish
Them safe return come spring to Balivanich,
The airport where his youngest Domhnall
Phadruig landed last, proud of his medal:
The Conspicuous Gallantry Cross for
Dicing with death, to build a bridge, under fire
In that 'Dreadful, dreadful place.' 'That shithole...'
Who can enlist to celebrate the soul
While others die in such a cause or Game?
Some thought I recall of Sorley MacLean.
Right or wrong. My course is set for Raasay,
The long way round. Tonight, Lochmaddie.
And here they are, the shooting party
Up from Hertfordshire – and suddenly
I'm MacNeice across the Minch of time
But upside down (and less adept at rhyme) –
A syndicate of builders bantering,
Waiting on their ghillie, reckoning
Their tally so far: a hundred grey-lag,
Four hundred golden plover... in the bag,
In the name of the island's economy.

Lost for words, I read in my pocket anthology
Highlands & Islands: Poetry of Place
Lines from Duncan Ban MacIntyre's 'In Praise
Of Ben Dorain' where deer and man
Become each other, lead each other on,
Body and soul in nature's mortal dance
Of being-in-the-world, beyond romance.
Romance the serpent in paradise,
Our folly ever to idealise.
'Art itself must have begun as nature'
Where the seen is rooted in matter... –
Says a piece in the *island news & ADVERTISER*
Where I find what holds the world together
('Comann na mara' Society of the Sea):
The Greylag Goose Management Committee;
Bagpipe Music at the College of Piping...
To say nothing of texting and skyping,
Hands across the sea, *O trompe l'oeil*:
So near, so far, again to say goodbye.
Now I've salt on my cheek and a rheumy
North-easterly eye, as we make for Skye
On a stiff crossing. There's spray on my lens.
So time's filtering of memory begins.

Now as agile as fingers on a chanter,
Keep note and let go. Forget to remember.
Remember to forget. Gulls keen and blaze
Beyond a dark night's window. I gaze
Through the shadows back into my head.
The crew ditch more fish-waste. The fire's fed
And Port Righ harbour's incandescent
Like a lighthouse lamp at some distant
Seamark. I lie in the dark and listen
To the ravenous din, as far back as I can,

Into my own wake, drowning in sleep,
Somewhere beyond the sea, right off the map…
Until woken by my notebook banging to the floor.
Now today stirs, soon to head for Sconser,
To catch the morning ferry Raasay-bound,
Its tense the future leaping like a hind.
Though 'Loch Striven', with no spring in her step,
Leaves elegance to the waves. See them leap
And bound at her shoulders, her raised car ramp,
Her short scut tracing an arc like chalk on damp
Slate this bleak grey morning of gusts and rain.
The Cuillins shape-shift, shadow and outline:
If Raasay didn't exist they'd have had to invent her
Just to be seen from Suishnish to Eyre,
Clachan to Fearns on the high hill road
But she has no need of any other world.
Inner or outer, self or other? Neither,
But one seamless presence, true to nature,
Green and sere and ripe now as the rowan,
Bejewelled with berries, about to spawn
Like a fish with eggs in golden gravel,
In Inverarish Burn, above a plunging pool.

I did not come by open boat to Raasay House
To walk the lawn and talk of other days;
But to see what the moment might discover.
'The skipper thinks he has seen you before,'
Says the ticket man. Am I from Greenock?
A man from HQ? Spying for Cal-Mac,
Making a promotion film towards a sell-off?
I laugh and wave goodbye. The sea runs rough.
The schoolchildren hurry from the bus
For the last sailing home. I try to guess
Their lives down the guttering winter days

To the year's turning and wilder seas.
Tomorrow I'll be back to guess again
But bound for Hallaig Wood in sun and rain
My route-march, solitary pilgrimage,
By wood and ridge to pay time homage.

I came there driven by more than passion
As far as North Fearns, by one Euan.
We talked of old feuds and sheep. Though my thoughts
Were of girls, coming and going, their ghosts
Metamorphosed into saplings. Until
On the verge below, as we ran downhill,
I saw a black woman like someone spectral
Out of Empire. Swaddled in her shawl,
A white infant. 'How are you?' Euan asked.
'Cold!… what do *you* think?' she laughed.
So far from Kenya, some TV wildlife
Presenter's nanny, sampling the wild life.
So times change and yet Raasay stands still,
Here above Inner Sound, and round the hill,
Below Beann na Leac, the plashy green way
To the poet's cairn, trig point to my day.

Art itself must have begun as nature.
Come in here. Take time. Take shelter.
Wait with only the wren for company
Under the green and dripping canopy.
Stand still. Gaze patiently. Acclimatise.
Absorb the world itself before your eyes.
Feel the weight of history on her knees:
The foursquare ruin, the silver-birch trees
All past child-bearing. And hidden somewhere,
Stock still with timeless stare, the deer.
Not outer but inner turned inside out,

Evicted, cleared into a green thought
As poignant as ever the poet dreamed
Of those girls. But now time the ferry claimed
Me away to the road, where the long climb
To Clachan rose, as if to kingdom come.
And on the tenth day I came down to Sleat
To Sabhal Mòr Ostaig where the elite
Stare down all English speech in stiff silence,
In age-old *ressentiment*'s deep grievance.
Higher above them, gazing out, not down,
Marxist, soldier, poet: Sorley MacLean.
What pressure on them, what future for their cause?
My privilege to hear their native noise.
What will happen? I sit and say nothing,
Inward at Ostaig. I think of running
Out a line in Welsh. But who'd understand?
So what will happen? I mean in Scotland
At fate's ballot box. Will heart or head decide?
Wear your heart on your sleeve. There is a tide,
You know, once taken will change history.
But god spare us your kilted-Tory monarchy.
Up the Republic! I say, heart on sleeve,
And praise the world for which I grieve.

Ten days on the road, as many weeks here
On the page. What better yield per hour
But to what end? That old thing-in-itself
Or something out beyond, in daily life?
Not either/or – but both? An 'I' speaking
To 'you' inspiring action from meaning?
It's not my call. Mine only to move on,
Zoom in and out, enjoy my delusion,
At the heart of recall, as the satellite
Picture shows what the weather's like tonight
Across the Minch or out in Barra Sound,

In Hallaig wood – my far-cry fishing ground,
My evermore and my *arrière-pays* –
My loss, it seems, deep-rooted in my DNA
Of which what's not Celtic is Norse Viking,
According to Professor Sykes. So scraping
My inner cheeks to help my sister know
Her paternal line gave me a glow...
Pulled me up short, to find my fate brought home –
Not by ferry or foot, but Y-chromosome –
To ponder strange facts, as if by sixth sense:
Instinct and conduct explained by science?
My descent's direct from 'The Tribe of Oisin'
With only a Viking or two in-between.
What does it mean? Answers on a postcard,
Photos of islands north-northwest preferred.
Meanwhile, my video software installed,
I replay my voyage, my hard disk filled
With the poetry of departure and arrival
To keep me on course and an even keel
As November closes down and winter
Raids in its wake, storming the harbour,
And with its aftermath of winnowed light
Redeems the moment and redeems the heart.
What is this solace we all crave, the loss
That cannot speak its name? No Paradise
On Earth. No Heaven. No Good Society
But that rode roughshod over some body
Of 'others' time and truth will bring to light
And in whose cause again stand up and fight.
Yet still we must hold fast and try to keep
Our heads above water – however steep,
However high it climbs, by peak and trough,
To drag us down – we must keep faith
In something like an island community
That knows the spring will come, and the ferry.

LIGHTHOUSE AT DAYBREAK

The coast clamoured at sea all night,
The island a meteor with a short wake
Flashing, warning and greeting.
Now come ashore, everywhere, as the early riser
The early tide, shoals to the gunwales.
Dear hearts and poor hearts blessed
Or bereaved, birthing and berthing
In the old round, find everything new today:
Waders in the surf-mouth wheeling
Jumble of weed and waste, trial and error,
What pays the rent and shapes the hour.

NIGHTWATCH

On the lonely back road when the stars were rising
Above the island and the ocean's nightwatch began
I passed myself coming back without a word between us
And not so much as a look from him of greeting
Though there was light enough to be seen.
How I remembered the world had once been
Beyond words and the day's mysterious business
Too vast and teeming to contend with for a moment.
My need shames me now for my blather
Who'd kept to himself so well all shades of thought
And dumb appetite for days hardly speaking.

NO VERSION OF PASTORAL

May no salt-of-the-earth or common touch
Contaminate your thought or speech.

CRITIQUE OF JUDGEMENT

And suddenly the view looks as though
An artist has been busy with her pastels,
Blunting the mountains and the hills
With mist of cloud and blue-green shadow:

Things for which god knows I'm a soft touch
No matter I can see through the gauze
To Nature red in teeth and claws
And hardship far beyond her crayon's reach.

This is what I call visionary appearance
To save me from the worst when I most need it
As when at any hour of day or night
I wake before pure reason's incoherence.

ON LOOKING INTO AN OLD PHOTOGRAPH

How being here leads home –
Never more heartfelt, the garden
And house seeming out of reach
Deep inland. *Here*, I protest again –
But bound north-northwest in mind
To a close horizon I might touch
With sea-light in the sky above
That promising unpromised land.

Will I ever visit you again my love?
I ask the view quietly in monochrome,
As I travel between pleasure deferred
And the pleasure of deferral,
Changing down to first from third,
To all but a halt on time's steep hill.

'THE SEA GOES ALL THE WAY ROUND THE ISLAND'

For they were long days, though short,
And short nights, though winter-long,
Rising before day into the deep thought
That is being, undistracted, like a song
In its tune, seamlessly one and the same.
As the man said: the sea goes all the way
Round the island. But here too like a half-rhyme,
Holm and home, headway and tideway,
Between compass-point and landmark
Asymmetric revelation does its work
And rounds the mind for another day.

ON THE ROCKS ROAD

There…

Preserve us I say
From narrow-gauge minds
But not narrow roads
With green spines
Where the heart's affections
Put best foot forward:
Between two stone walls
Built to the rhythm
Of rock-form and contour
Of labour and time
Straight as a die
Dipping in and out of sight
Opening and narrowing
Ahead behind – behind ahead
In threadbare karst country

Grown where nothing grows
Better than light and lichen
Rare alpine, common thorn,
Atlantic gale and storm
Limestone, stone by stone
Advancing to delay
To the last angle and oval
With makeshift-erratic
Punctuation of granite
Relief work in stark relief –
As now at home recalling
I step up from Cill Rónáin
Over the top and down
To Gort na gCapall (a.k.a. West Cork)
The field of the horse
On my solitary walk
Unpicking as I go
The old formula:
Distance over speed and time –
Beyond recognition
In my mind-body economy
Of presences and memory
In and out of step
Balancing line on line
Not carelessly picked
Or casually piled
But as those men worked
With steady eye and hand.
But hold your step
As the Rocks Road
Has ever done
Since it began
Never to travel its own length
Nor time its progress

Never to see but to be
From end to end
Its centre of gravity where
But here and there?
In infinite recession
Beyond the sum of knowledge
Beyond botany book
And guide to birds
Studies of fossils
Or place-names
In the folds of a map
And where the wild rose
Blows in nothing's name.
What do I bring?
Nothing it knows.
What do I take?
Nothing it will miss.
Where am I bound?
To the field of the horse.

And back...

As now I am again
Stepping out of time
Working my way in
From the port
Of the fort's mouth
Through a giant jetsam
Of rock and boulder
Beside which sea-wall
The village of the horse takes shelter
Itself an island in a sea of stone
Safe as houses but no safer
As a FOR SALE sign tells

Wired to a garden gate
The rogee Time at work
Waiting on the highest bidder
No safer than mortality:
The O'Flaherty home
Of radical fame.
A story to be told there
But to the stranger more
One of stage directions
With pauses and no text between
Where no one seems to live
But when the little bus comes round
A woman disembarks
With shopping bags from 'SUPERMAC'S'
To disappear indoors
And at evening an old man
Emerges to Flymo the lawn
And two brothers further on
Look up startled as
I take them by surprise
Calling as I go: 'Fine evening!'
And at once bend back
To hack at briars
As if lifetimes ago
Drifting into silence behind me
In deepening shadow
As the day fades
And evening sharpens
To monochrome
Then dims to a glimmer of lights
Beside the sea's fire
And the nightwatch begins
Behind drawn curtains
Via dish and aerial

As I start the steep climb
Back the way I came
Out of sight out of mind
Out of mind into vision
And I pass myself
Coming back in silence
The way not the same
My step different
Though not my passion
For the Rocks Road.
Do not ask life's purpose
But live every step of the road
(The time it takes knows
Nothing of distance or speed)
In the world of matter
And mind brought together
As in making's invention
I write this for you:
Call it ordinariness
Call it best of all love
As the walls ahead touch
At their vanishing point
And keep opening.

CORMORANT

The sea's too big for the cormorant's digestion,
Yet it grabs it in its beak, flashing and scaled.
Baptism by fire its routine, then total immersion.
On neither count has it so far failed
The old argument from experience to resurrection.

Remember, nothing in Nature but man is cursed.
And take heart for every day truth stands revealed
Beyond the beholder, as long as life might last,
Glinting like a weather-vane above the Seaman's Mission,
A starry riding-light atop a pitching mast.

PORT SHEÁNIA REVISITED

The hooded crows work on ahead
Combing the tidemark in no-man's-land.
Wind flutters their brief flights to avoid me.
So places travel on the spot to and fro
And round and away in the heart's wake.
The cormorants hang out on table rock
As ever at low tide, drying their wings,
Digesting both species of pollack and
Squirting out a gouache of honeyed shit.
Curlew and oystercatcher compare notes
On a scale of limpidity beyond reckoning.
Two eggs in a tern-scrape of pebble and shell
Have become three since yesterday.
No one comes here any more to disturb them,
To harvest sea-candles or periwinkles
Nor an armful of driftwood for the fire.
This goes on all day, all night, without human agency.
Why should that not console me?

HARBOUR INN

The sea wants for nothing yet is all lack…
What enchants me here I chant
To its hunger, its drunken slap and smack.

Its chain-link rattle, as the day's slant
Grey goes reeling, with highlight
Of gannet, gull, and white-horse mane,
Rain on stone, on slate, and skylight,
Out there beyond the window-pane.

Where the ferry's making heavy weather
As if caught mid-Sound in a painting.
See how it wallows, treading water.
Who knows whether it's coming or going?
Surely the folk in here know
Who as to souls in peril and distress
Keep one eye on the clock's slow
Hands, the other on their glass.

ON NOT SAILING TO ST KILDA

The windows shut against the weather,
I climbed the hill through bog and heather.

I saw a golden eagle and a mountain hare
And found an antler of a deer.

I walked along Hushinish shore
And watched a gannet plunge down ice-cold air.

All in a southeast wind I saw forever
Nothing to my mind that might repair

The dream of sailing to St Kilda
As I had dreamt it months before.

A RETURN OF THE NATIVE

And this comes to its end, not to be met with again,
Though weather and season make the best match they can
Tuning wind and rain and the sea-lit dawn
And not everyone has passed on and some return
But time has taken them and what they were is gone
Into the depths of heart and mind towards oblivion
But for love's last hold on her companion reason
Sustained by epiphanies on hope's frugal pension
Against what cannot now be done, or undone.

REQUIEM

'It was damnable.'
Ivor Gurney

I

Night blooms shadows among clouds like damaged lungs.
Oban's carry-outs are busy and spring is in the offing.
Men in half-lit wheelhouses prepare for the night's fishing.
Smokers hang in doorways bleakly staring, cold, hooked on last-gasp cigs
Like conscripts about to go over the top to certain death,
Or disaffected sentries. The Esplanade imagines things in monochrome
With patrician soundtrack from Pathé, or footage from 'Atlantic Convoy'.
In the cockpit of my top-floor hotel room I stare at my instrument panel:
Paper, pen and ink – and chart my next sortie. No dead reckonings
On the muse's missions just the waste of waters and the hit or miss
Of chance, abandonment more in the spirit of that Irish airman
Than anything anyone in the squadron entertained
Though some on foot, like Douglas, knew what the poet intended.
So-and-so had a 'good war' (discuss). A war by any other name...
Many strange meetings. The other night after dinner

The Brigadier sat next to me wept as the port went round.
I saw him with my own eyes in the blur of subdued light.
He kept on talking while the tears ran down his high-boned cheeks.
It might have been a scene at Craiglockhart long ago.
'We have yet to understand what "collateral" means for this generation,'
One remarked next day as to PTSD; and I had already seen,
Startling awake, struggling for air, my son stood over me,
The night before, a foot taller than he is wherever he is 'semi-feral…'
'On a recce call-sign' by Helmand River. Six weeks and not a word.
Neither love nor fear can tolerate a vacuum. But how soft we are
Compared with then. I mean the *durée* in 'the duration'.
So many silences at the heart of battle resounding as if to eternity.
('We will remember them.') The reach of suffering lost in action
As invasive as water by the Somme.
Then the knock at the door and the shadow beyond it.

2

It was evening. The garden sodden with winter, hawthorn's stark crown
Against the last of a December day. I came in and opened my inbox, idly,
On the *qui vive* and there found at last my 'Field (Service) Post Card'
Slipped in on the ether under cover like a star into a dark night.
'Our early weeks there were dominated by close-quarter engagements.'
A thrill of armchair courage and pride like the curse of a general's

                                                    strategy,

A politician's lie (imperious white lie), ran through my veins,
Or was it mere relief made the hair on the back of my neck stand
To hurried attention, as if late on parade? Then the thought came to me.
Free-verse is war epitomised: strict drill, routines blown apart
Revealing fault-lines, fracturing up the chain of command
Where the sergeant-major struts up and down before a parade of ghosts.
Hear him barking pentameters and dactyls, bristling
Like a demented German shepherd, his masters whistling for him
In the European dark, joint-winners of the Nobel Prize for Peace.
Insurgent or fanatic, military success but political failure, victory or

Defeat. Tick the boxes according to preference, you 'pernicious race
Of little odious vermin' as the general's horse whinnied under his breath
Prancing on the parade ground, clopping, jingling, his nibs
In full ceremonial jackboots and cuirass, the works, muttering
Honi soit qui mal y pense, a grenadier whistling snatches from 'Lillibulero'.
Pomp and circumstance. Hearts and minds. Tell it to: 'The likely INS,
The spies, the elderly one-time mujahadin'. Tell it to: 'The barefoot girl
No older than seven walking her cow through plashy ice-cold fields'.
Tell it to the marines that their fallen comrades did not die in vain.
Tell it to the hardy Helmundi Pashtuns who saw off the Russians
And now the airhead Romans of the western empire, empty-handed
Back where they came from, their cover stories already ghosted for them.
Tell it to the poppy fields, and the opiate of Remembrance Day.
Tell it any way you like but know nothing humanity touches is true quite.

3
I stood with the townspeople, observed the silence, the laying of wreaths,
By the various causes and worthies, the WI, the local Masonic Lodge,
Heard the last post and watched their faces, solemn, respectful,
Trying to imagine my own among them, one of many –
More than ever, in recent memory, they said – but distracted in thought
By the earlier talk of men near me, one or two campaign medals apiece,
On faded ribbons, and younger men with more, perhaps for bravery,
And this old falangist of Queen and Country, retired from the Met,
Speaking of Sovereignty and Treachery and the 'Heart of England',
His 'group' at work studying Constitutional Law with a view to bringing
Charges of Treason against Blair and Cameron on the question of Europe.
And the others listening inscrutably, without dissent, staring, not a hint
Of a smile or disbelief, their worlds their remembrance what?
Elsewhere in the crowd how many thinking of their own flesh and blood
In harm's way as winter bites into Helmand and farmers harvest at last,
Crops to them, cover to the fighters, and in each feuding village
Rival calls to prayer resound along the river and if you close your ears
The countryside but for its compounds and the cold might be somewhere

In rural Kent or Suffolk at the height of autumn, but for the seven-year-old
Circling round on a motorbike with five- and three-year-old siblings
On the pillion, but for the patrols, the air strikes, the horror, the horror.
And the roll call of lives claimed with nothing to say of what's in a name.
And the policy pronouncements a paper trail beyond oblivion
Come out of nowhere like a sudden enemy, a thief in the night of reason.
And when I woke up in the morning like one who made it back
From a night-sortie, combing the waves for a flare, for a signal
At the edge of sound, billeted at 'The Great Western' or 'The Esplanade',
'The Alexandra' or 'The Marine', nothing was any the clearer
But the cold air as I drew up the sash-window ran clean through me
And I was as if not there… the ink now dry in my name and 'permanent'.

ROUND ABOUT A GREAT ESTATE

Eat your heart out in cavernous envy
Capability. Fold up the Estate map and put away
The plantation, the marsh, the bridleway,
The shooting box, the loch, the little jetty,
The fish-trap chevrons down the estuary –
Likenesses lost in divine disarray, the key
Locked on the old order and authority,
The cult of breeding and its ascendancy.
The PRIVATE keep-out and man-trap tyranny
Of that ancien régime of cut-glass barbarity.
The photographs of staff and tenantry,
Their story in Sunday-best for posterity
Recycled now as heritage and legacy:
The guns with their bag, keeper and ghillie,
Stalker and stag, the whisky distillery,
Captain of cavalry, captain of industry –
The whole shooting match and gallimaufry:

A seat in the House, a seat in the country,
Every conceivable hierarchy and cliché
Shored up by portfolios of gilts and property.
Blow to the four corners your grandeur and folie
Careers in Whitehall, careers at the Embassy.
Blow too what passes for your mind: the sea
Mocks in its rock garden, mocks the gently
Falling landscapes that border so privately
Their framed view, crying out to beauty,
The seven-sided sea, with its sails full of sky.
Hear the wintry roar of its eternal battery.
Observe its genius for blunt-sheared topiary
And closest nail-scissor trim in sandy
Border, and marvel you ever had your day
Between home and far-flung colony.
Put off your self. Walk the margin of the bay,
O heir to the ruin of all you survey.

SHORE LEAVE

Turn your back on it and walk away
Until the sea's a distant memory only
Woken by inland gulls and the tidal
Rush of a motorway's perpetual
Arrival-and-withdrawal, windborne
For miles to break about town
And village, islanded farmstead,
Distant parish church with its dead
Run aground below, under headstone
After headstone in the short tide
Poppy-wreath adrift beneath the War Memorial.

AT THE LANDFILL SITE

I lose my way in misfortune
Between the epic and the everyday:
My voyage and little history
Like the swan in the street
The albatross on deck
Out of their element:
The fox at the landfill site.
Gulls set alight
Over bonfire seas of garbage.

I was turned back at the gate
Directed to an entry down the road
Reserved for books and manuscripts.
It seemed I drove for many years.
Waste management was ever
The work of third parties.
Is nothing true and nothing sacred
But what they happen to recycle?
I pulled in off the road and slept.

Once I turned and saw a ghost
Behind me on a lakeside road.
Now I startled at seeing him again.
'The journey from darkness into darkness…'
His dumb lips mouthed
But then he faded.
The trucks of waste tailed back beyond
Orange lights strobing into littered thorn.
I filled my notebook with another poem.

NET MENDING

Who hasn't been there, up against the wall,
untangling feelings; with line and needle
stitching rent and hurt, back into squares
and make-do diamonds, running repairs
to heart and mind, with one eye on the tide-table,
the other on the ink-black sky? Making
ends meet to keep going. Thinking
but not needing to say, 'Oh let's not quarrel
with our luck or blame the weather. Nothing
will come of that but more of the same.'
Take heart, I say, idling by the harbour
with pen and paper, ever on course for
fair or foul weather, the storm still reeling
after its night on the tiles, the sea aflame.

CORNCRAKE AGAIN

Stitching along unseen:
the invisible mender
of our broken nature,
between now and then.

NOWHERE IN-BETWEEN

I know the way back
doesn't lead there
or anywhere quite

I've been before:
a scene in a book
or play, a chapter,
where fortunes take
a better turn or worse.
I think I remember
but we remember only memories.

Nowhere in-between
is exactly true.
So open the book,
go through it again,
and tell me when you do
what conclusions
you come to now
and what you know
given that to know
is only to resemble.

A VISIT

I went to see him. He was old then
and laughed at what he forgot and found
as if out of thin air, his mind elsewhere.
The ground floor flat not anywhere
he'd call home but where he lived happily enough.
It had never been the plan. And yet to me
the books, the tall window and the view,
the few paintings, landscapes by his wife,
and by his daughter, his eagerness for me
to listen with him for more than an hour
to Shostakovich's '24 Preludes & Fugues'
seemed an idyll of an enviable kind, a script

I'd write for myself for when things fall apart
piecemeal like that late autumn afternoon.
He'd showed me what he'd kept, letters from
great poets he'd known, old photographs
of himself and X, and Y, some manuscripts
that had come his way, his own books
and those by others in his long-gone world.
The rest he said was archived somewhere,
which seemed to cut him short, until suddenly:
'Dying is for the living,' he exclaimed, keenly,
something he liked to say, 'There's no future
in posterity.' I'd heard the same before, and
'Never look to be wise. Speak your mind.
Wisdom is for fools.' And then he rose
that we should neither outstay his welcome.
A bloom of wine hung in my lungs long after
I got home and his talk of Cold War days
ran on like a newsreel in my head until
that flicker and flap as the spool reaches its end
and I sat on a moment in the dark, moved
by a sudden understanding of my life.

HOMECOMING

I came there, cap in hand,
as if a beggar to the day
or reverent soul before his maker.

I wish I could have stayed away
for the change I found there
and the change in me.

I SEE ORION

I see Orion out tonight patrolling our western flank.
By midnight he'll be just round the corner of our row
heading off like clockwork, wound up long ago,
his silver epaulettes still bright enough to make me blink

as I stand here on a cold March night, bedazzled by
what isn't there and never moves except
the heart, to the kind of wonder nothing can buy.
One of those moments when treasure you've kept

hoarded from time comes to light again. And rest
my soul, whatever that means, I'm blessed
once more and starry-eyed, before beauty –
moved to see it again as a new discovery.

If not as it used to be when I faced this way in youth
far off in time and space and knew the truth.

SEA-GARDEN

Here she is westering into spring,
her winter rigging still bare –
her power subterranean,
tidal turning over unseen
as she tugs and clacks at mooring
and the thrush begins to sing.

Now trim the climbing rose
and do not jib to haul her close
the better to raise more sail
as the evenings start to fail

later and later and bridal
wake of white unfurls to green.

Until at last it's time to sit out late
on course for the solstice
where today dallies with tomorrow,
and on the rocks means with ice –
all our troubles stowed below,
waiting for the sun to set.

HARVESTS

I stood there deep in memory, staring long ago,
as harvest time rattled round the upland farms
sickle-bars chattering, reels whirling
and knotted sheaves falling in the stubble
for shocking into stooks and shadows.

You could see the clattering shore from up there too
and the reaper round the rocks
making the last cut over and over
in the blinding stubble there –
the chopping waves, the sheaves and stooks of light.

Here were no parables or lessons drawn from life
about the melancholy passing of time,
no sentiment or nostalgia-in-waiting,
no carpe diem, just a proposition
about two scenes like each other and unlike.

WARNING TO READERS

Mind the gap between
the poem and the quay.

NOTES FROM AN ISLAND

1
Now she's the wrecked ship, blown on to herself, stoved and
    broken below the waterline, sea thundering in hold and
    engine room. Wind howling through her.
Kilmartin retired coxwain tends his bar as once the lifeboat.
    Satellite TV for Satnav. The fortunes of Man U dearest to
    him.
Steady as he goes, in Ferguson's wake, quietly serving
    his regulars. Old hands. Experts in silence. The oldest
    language of all, hardest to learn. Now little heard, only a
    handful of native speakers surviving.

2
Keep a steady hand on the wheel of your thoughts. Keep a
    steady hand on hope, the island says as it rides the storm.
Hear it through the floorboards of your heart, the broken
    window panes.

3
A stranded funeral party, ties loosened, sits murmuring into
    the small hours.
They linger catching up, expanding on the past. Then brave
    it out, to stagger half-drowned, groping for their beds,
    as if underwater, the search for survivors called off until
    daylight.

4
Time now in the night's wake
For a new poem on your breakfast plate:

Not silence but quiet
the word held mid-air
a shell to your ear
slightest decibels of light
a keening gull
tangible as salt.

Wader-notes calling to
waves that won't break
and the folk down to wait
for the boat, their talk
as old as fate, still
of tragedies and omens.

There is no doubt the tides
are getting higher.
Year on year they rock the boat
ever nearer and nearer
the constellations
and the Cyclops moon.

5
She lists today, shouldering her burden, shipping cloud, leaning to
windward, her bow waves high, her scuppers awash as the sea
races by from the west.

Not that we'll make anywhere before night, other than where we
are, port and starboard righting themselves as the wind drops
anchor.

6

I tried the other life, he said, but I prefer this one.
Less being more I chose to dream small,
and so you find me here; what you call 'a local',
trying to make a different kind of fortune.

Still I could leave, if I wanted to... you know?
But it's all to lose now, my being here
for its own sake, my being here for the like of you
to chat with on your holidays each year.

Me with my stories of fishing and drowning –
if there'll ever be mackerel again in the autumn;
if the weather doesn't break to bring
winter early and who knows what to come –

The same old patter, tinged with sorrow and regret,
seeing yourself there – with your wife
and children, in your summer clothes... trying to forget
the long off-season at the heart of life.

7

If you have nowhere to get to, and like to have some fishing to look
     at, wait by the slipway in the far west. And you'll see them come
     in.
Or they'll pass you on the road in that rust-bucket car humming
     with the smell of fish, lobster-bait, and the soak of the sea.
You lost sight of them on the hill down, hugging the shore of the
     small islands. You lost sight of them between peak and trough.
But they are there in the old intimacy, speaking the old language.
     Don't be misled by the outboards and the mobile's ship-to-
     shore.
Nothing's altered that yet, though nothing assuages the sea.

8

Pockets of it up here now where you'll still hear it spoken in the
light karst country dialect, so nuanced and accented, loved by
so many.

Spell-binding. Mind-healing.

And if you come again in spring you should just make out the
purest corncrake, assimilated, committed to memory.

Letter 'C' in the local lexicon soon to expand further with the
Silence for: chough and curlew. Subject to final confirmation
from observers in the field.

9

In the end they settled in Salthill. He wrote to say, 'I can see
Ceann Boirne at the end of the Burren from my bedroom
window. I could see it also from my bedroom at Bárr a Phointe,
but from a different angle.'

Surely that ought to be enough for anyone in life's adjustments.
Even in the mind's eye and far away it might suffice, even on a
bad day of low cloud.

10

Then Bartley showed them where the two Viking youths were
buried, close inside the wall of the Dún, in the foetal position,
the one seeming to whisper in the ear of the other as he nursed
him in his lap.

What's the Old Norse for silence?
How old is time? I have forgotten.

11

The three Connemaras in the lonely meadow above the Summer
   School nearly speak it like natives now but every so often they
   fall back on their mother tongue, seamlessly, without realising
   what they're doing as they hear hoof-beats somewhere on the
   far road.

Houyhnhmn houyhnhmn they whinny tossing their long heads at
   the dappled sky.

12

Oh the rational life!

When he saw the light, he left the Order. Then he married and
   came back from Africa. There was nothing about prayer he
   didn't know, in several languages, from Irish to Sanskrit. He'd
   taught the Koran to children in Dar-es-salaam.

When the diagnosis numbered his days, they came together to
   settle in his birthplace, what the islanders call 'The Rock'.

13

On that still morning he wrote in his note-book:

The island hasn't moved an inch
since I stepped over her side.

But many are her losses since
among those I left behind

steering their course
on time's indifferent tide.

LUNCH WITH SEAMUS

I saw him hurry by a hotel window where I sat
nursing time over a steadying glass
before I went along to keep our assignation
at Doyle's, a few yards away. Bloomsbury
seemed to suit him, and I thought as I thought
of MacNeice in October and said to myself
this is the life. Not our first time
but first time *tête à tête* and both of us I think
uncertain how lunch might pass *Chez Gerrard*,
the occasion to mark his pamphlet *A Shiver*.

I'll tell you now, we got on like a house on fire.
A turf fire too, burning underground,
through worlds in common, though mine
much second-hand from my father's time,
with North Clutag steading called to mind,
the Hill Head, the smithy, the far moss...
A common universe slowly synchronising
helped by a bottle he paused to praise.
Reckless now I asked would he read
a new poem I'd done set by the Súile.

'Slower,' he smiled when slowly he'd finished,
'A slow air.' Now animated, he leaned
closer and said, intimately, as if in confession:
'*This* is what I like. This is how it used to be.
Usually now if I go to lunch like this they sit
silent, waiting for the oracle to speak.'
I reined myself in, now he had his head.
'I got the Nobel Prize too soon,' he said.
'It nearly did for me, you know, the fame.
It stops the clock and steals your time.
Shall I say, it made the electric light flicker...?'

As if on cue, a young man with a piece of paper
rose from a table nearby, to beg an autograph.
I watched him sign. His hand at once caught my eye,
I mean the hand itself, a small hand,
for a big mind, born for the pen,
unbruised by past spade-work or other labour.
By now it was fast approaching four
and with the bit between my teeth I offered
to take him fishing. He looked at me, as if in pity:
'You know, I never did it, but only saw it done.'

Eye to eye we met and his canny look
made me think again the nature of the man.
I felt as if sobered into reality, by the redress
of poetry, what might be done by merely
seeing things, if you are Seamus Heaney.
But now the place was empty but for us
and the waiters wanted us gone.
We parted and I watched him disappear
as if I'd dreamt the whole affair
but knowing I hadn't. I'd seen the man.

AURA OF WINTER

We had a prowler last night
an uninvited guest in the garden.

No tell-tale footprint or snapped twig
just a colder breath to the morning

and the ribbon of mist across the field
broken where he came and went.

A POET: 21ST CENTURY

A redundant lighthouse-keeper
striking a match in a storm.

WELSH INTERVAL

at Penmon Point

The lighthouse tolls its warning bell
tolls and tolls again in Easter's wake.
Cold easterlies off the mountains bite
as the grey generations, menfolk
tonsured by time, leave their cars
and take a turn along the shingle's
limestone glare, in knifing ozone,
with more than half a mind on lunch.

What is it about an island scene
that meets our longing for completion?
Across the waves the bell carries
time to its mark and back again
as it has done as many times
as there are pebbles here or more:
night and day, star for star, pulsing
of perils and mortality.

It asks perhaps who's counting,
to admonish us, and who hears,
and what do we hear? Not a bell
but *egwyl* – a Welsh interval –
the voice of silence, a Zen koan
answer-and-no-answer. Time held

in mid-air. Clang… A sound
both still and silent. Clang…

A marine and monkish moment
speaking to what we never had:
a life at sea, a life of prayer
in a language we can only hear
not comprehend. Just as, unoccupied,
the coastguard cottages
appear to stare at Puffin Island
as if waiting for something to happen.

MEDITATION IN PATERNOSTER SQUARE

The city sails in snow and the citizens
breast and brave it as they wouldn't
under rain, smiling at imperfect strangers,
partners in a reel who've yet to learn
the steps. And I'm here at my usual game
at which I am inch-perfect, melancholy
reflection before a glass of wine.
With one eye on my pen, the other
on that ode by Horace addressed
to Fortune and the fate of Rome, I brood,
past and present on my mind, here and
there in this bar in Paternoster Square
soaking up the atmosphere of City folk
at play in Christmas hats like crowns.
Hostages all to the snow outside and
to the crunch and freeze of assets.
What do I care at my time, almost home
and dry, that the pillars shudder? I took
no oath to anything unless to push my pen,

against the eternal enemies; and not
to starve – just like any soldier at his outpost
locked in the iron grip of time, wherever
my verses go, before the wine runs dry.
Here, in furthest snow-garbed Britain
I sip and think of Horace and Augustus,
dwelling on rule and misrule, fortune's
wheel, the horror left undone, by St Paul's
sailing through snow all afternoon.

BROKEN LINE OR MICHAEL MULDOON'S LAMENT

Though spring came roughly on time
within a week of the North wind dying
and I waited for them as usual,
they never arrived, or never set out
for the island, or perished en route.
Even as May passed
I held out hope as June advanced.

But they didn't come, and missing a generation
never came again – the line broken.
It's been hard ever since never to hear them.
To loiter all evening
and not catch a glimpse of one
though that was often the way
even when they were here.

WRITER'S BLOCK

The year's keel heeling in harbour mud,
several degrees from upright. Neap tide
= sun, moon, earth at right angles,
to gauge our kilter by. Days ashore
submarine, pent and cabin-fevered.
Nights ocean-wide but frugally lit,
as if with energy-saving stars.
Uncharted mind-games in lubberdom,
pending a new part, or a total refit?
He can barely remember when he last set out,
no more than when he came back
except the engine failed and he was towed
with next-to-nothing in his hold.
Now he frets and frays at a loose end
while for others the fishing is good.

RICHARD MURPHY

Between our roads, a handful of years,
and then the past all round these shores
haunted by the ghost of the *Ave Maria*
telling the epic of the Cleggan Disaster,
holding today up to yesterday's mirror –
the world kept afloat by running repairs.

The landlady of Oliver's Seafood Bar
calls – from a tale or song of long ago? :
'Your heart beats when you hear my name,'
she laughs and tells it him again, 'Joe, Joe,
your heart beats when you hear my name.'
So Cleggan resounds, the day set fair

waiting for the ferry. And my head full
of memories of sailing to an island –
of corncrakes in the month of June
grinding out their tuneless tune:
such unlikely music. My heart unmanned
to hear it once more, to hear it still

on Inishbofin by Cromwell's fort
and the blind tower, as the ferry departs
and leaves me caught in '68 and '69 again,
days on the cusp of violence as they were,
reminded of all those broken hearts
from 'Droit de Seigneur' to Aughrim –

holding yesterday up to today's mirror
and reading in its guilt-edged frame
the old story of a poet's prescience
who saw tomorrow the day before.
Small wonder then that I should say:
my heart beats when I hear his name.

THINKING OF JONAH

If I could say it took the metaphor
out of my sails, I might make my way.

The scales fall from the waves.
The lucky man lives

to tell his tale
thinking of Jonah in the whale.

That much I can hold on to, as to an oar
rotating on its thole-pin, between air and water.

I hear the creak and rattle of it, the knock
and racket of putting my back into it.

My mind to it. I cannot hear the high Atlantic
being under it, being above it.

I know one day it will swallow me whole
and I'll swim in the belly of the whale.

And the helter-skeltering stars
will count the years on the tips of their fingers.

INTIMACIES

And so we sit here for a while together,
an ancient couple in their gazebo
revisiting old truths in a glass or two,
making the most of freak warm weather.

We do what we can with what we have
written through us, and what we dream,
we dream, or run to ground in stolen time
like this, those intimacies for which we live.

Searching for sense in a crazy world –
bewildered by too much information,
sidelined by the techno generation,
their devices no sooner new than old.

Their lives a solipsism where means are ends,
where speed and scale are deities,
hubristic billionaires dictate new pieties
and folk they've never met are friends.

All of whom are called and all chosen
and who would argue with that
or risk going viral among the trolls? And yet
it still remains what's odd can never be even.

We pour another glass, each to their tipple.
The evening light begins to thin and fail.
House martins dart announcing their arrival.
We wonder for another year at this miracle of April.

Until I start up about the rise of Islam.
The cue for you to totter down the lawn
knowing that very soon I'll move on
to my party piece about the fall of Rome.

THE BATTLE OF MALDON

from the Anglo-Saxon [1]

         …   would be broken.
He bade each warrior   leave his horse
to drive it far off   to go forward
plan deeds of arms   steadfast courage.
Then Offa's kinsman   as soon as he saw
the earl would not   conscience cowardice
let his loved one   fly from his hand

---

1 Translated during the Brexit referendum furore.

hawk to holt   and advanced to fight
so man might know   this youth would not
weaken in battle   once he took up arms.
Ealdric too   began to advance
spear to battle   would serve his chief
his lord in the fight   while he might
steadfast in mind   hold in hand
shield and broadsword   fulfil his vow
before his lord   when he must fight.

There Byrhtnoth   lined up his men
rode before them   ordered his warriors
how to stand   what place to hold
to bear their shields   fast in hand
without fear.   When he had his folk
properly arrayed   he dismounted among them
among his most   devoted hearthmen
where it pleased him most to be.

Then stood on the shore   a Viking messenger
called out sternly   threatening words
a message from the Vikings   to the earl
'Bold seamen sent me to you   ordered me to say
that you must quickly send   rings for protection.
It's better for you   to buy off this spear-storm
than that we should   join bitter battle
no need to destroy each other.   If you are prosperous
we will confirm   peace with gold.
If you who are richest here   decide you will
pay ransom   for your people
hand over to seamen   money of their choosing
in return for truce   and take peace from us
we will board ship   with tribute-money
go to sea   and keep peace with you.'

Byrhtnoth raised his shield   high
brandished his slender ash-spear   spoke words
wrathful and resolute   gave him answer
'Hear you seaman   what these folk say?
They will give you   spears for tribute
deadly spear-point   sword tried and tested
war-gear   that won't profit you in battle.
Seamen's messenger   deliver this in reply
tell your people   a much more hateful message
that here stands   a dauntless earl with his troop
who will defend   their homeland
Æthelred's country   land of my lord
folk and ground.   Heathens must
fall in battle.   Too shameful it seems to me
that you should board ship   with our tribute
without a fight now you've come   thus far into our land.'

                    * * *

He ordered them   bear shields and advance.
Now they stood fast   on the river bank,
halted by water   flood after ebb
currents surging   barring battle.
It felt too long   before they might fight.
By Pante's stream   they stood proud
men of Essex   facing off the Viking fleet.
Neither side   could harm the other –
except arrow's flight   might deal death.
The flood went out.   The Vikings stood ready,
many Vikings   eager for battle.
He ordered the heroes   to hold the causeway.
One called Wulfstan   stern in fight
of valiant kin   Ceola's son
killed the front man   with his first spear

held his ground boldly   there at the bridge.
There stood with Wulfstane   warriors undaunted
Aelfere and Maccus   two bold men
who would not take flight   from that ford
but stoutly stood   against the enemy
for as long as they might   weapons wield.
When they saw   and saw clearly
what bitter opposition   they met at the causeway
those hateful strangers   began to use guile.
They asked for passage   to land to lead
their foot-soldiers   over the ford.

Then Byrhtnoth   in his overweening pride
gave those hateful people   too much ground.
And Byrththelm's son   began to call
over the cold water   (warriors listened)
'Now the way is open   come to us quickly
men to war   God alone knows
who might   master this battlefield.'
Slaughterwolves advanced   recked not water
the Viking band   west over Pante
over gleaming water   bore shields
seamen to land   with shields of linden.
There against the foe   stood ready
Byrhtnoth with his warriors   ordered them make
a battle-hedge of shields   and hold fast
against the enemy.   Then the fight was near
glory in battle.   The time was come.
Doomed men must fall   wounded or dead.
Clamour rose   ravens circled for carrion
eagles cried.   There was uproar on earth.
Sharp file-hardened spears   flew from hands
bows were busy   shields met spear-points.

Bitter the rush of battle.   Warriors fell.
On either side   young men lay dead.
Wulfmaer was wounded.   Byrhtnoth's sister's son
cruelly hacked with swords   met death in battle.
There were the Vikings   made to pay.
I heard that Eadweard   so fiercely struck one
with his sword   held nothing back
that he fell at his feet   a doomed warrior
for which his lord   gave thanks
to his chamberlain   when he had a chance in mid-fray.
They stood firm   resolute
young warriors in battle   thought how
they might be first   with spear-points
to destroy men   to conquer life
warriors with weapons.   The slain fell to earth.
They stood steadfast.   Byrhtnoth ordered
each young warrior   to be of single mind
win glory in battle   against the Danes.
Then one battle-hardened   weapon raised
shield at the ready   stepped up.
So the earl   advanced on the churl
each to the other   intending harm.
Then the sea-warrior   sent a spear (of southern make)
that wounded   the warriors' lord
who shoved with shield   shivered the shaft
so the broken spear   sprang back.
Enraged, the warrior   stung with spear
the proud Viking   who'd wounded him.
Wise was the warrior.   He passed his spear
through the young man's neck   hand-steered it
fatally pierced   his sudden attacker.
Then speedily   he pierced another
so his chain-mail burst   wounded him
in the breast   through the linked rings

the deadly point   stood in his heart.
The earl was the happier   and laughed
a courageous man   thanked god
for the day's work   the Lord gave him.

Then a Viking warrior   sent a spear speeding
from his hand   so that it sped
through the noble   Æthelred's liegeman.
Stood by his side   a young warrior not fully grown
a youth in battle who   very valiantly
plucked from the warrior   the bloody spear
Wulfstan's son   the young Wulfmaer
threw it back   with exceeding force in reply
pierced   the one who'd thrown it
so that now he lay on earth   who had
so grievously   reached his lord before.

Then an armed man approached   said to the earl
he would for this   carry off rings
spoils and treasure   ornamented sword.
Then Byrhtnoth drew   sword from sheath
broad and gleaming   struck the corslet.
But too quick to stop him   the Viking
wounded the earl   in the arm.
Fell then to earth   golden-hilted sword
nor might he hold fast   the hard sword
weapon wield.   Still the hoary old warrior
spoke   encouraged young warriors
bade them go forward   advance stoutly together
nor might he stand   any longer.
He looked to the heavens :
'I thank the Lord   ruler of people
for all joys I've had   in the world.
Now I own, merciful God   greatest good

that you grant my spirit   all that is good
that my soul might   journey to you
into your power   lord of angels
go in peace.   I am entreating you
that the fiend from hell   might not harm it.'

Then the heathen warriors   killed him
and both men who'd   stood by him
Ælfnoth and Wulfmaer   both lay slain
close by their lord   gave their lives.
Then they retreated   who didn't want to be there.
There was Oddan's son   first to flee
Godric from battle   and abandon that good man
who'd given him often   many a steed.
He leapt on a horse   that had belonged to his lord
on the trappings   to which he had no right
and his brother with him   both galloped
Godwine and Godwig   cared not for battle
but went from the fight   and sought the wood
fled to that fastness   and saved their lives
and more men   than was befitting
were they to remember   all the favours
he had granted   to their benefit.
So Offa had said   earlier that day
in the hall   where they met
that many there   spoke boldly
who'd not endure   when needed later.

                    * * *

There was fallen   the people's lord
Æthelred's earl.   His closest followers
all saw   that their lord lay dead.
Then they advanced   proud liegemen

undaunted men   hastened eagerly.
Then would they all   do one of two things
leave life   or else be avenged.
So they exhorted   Ælfrice's son to advance
warrior young in winters   spoke words
then Ælfwine said   spoke valiantly.
'I remember the speeches   often made at meed
when sat on benches   we boasted loudly
heroes in hall   concerning bitter battle.
Now you might   prove who's brave.
I will make known   my descent
that I was close kin   of the Mercians
my grandfather   was called Ealhelm
wise nobleman   of worldly prosperity.
Nor among the people   shall liegemen reproach me
that I shall   desert this army
head for home   now my lord lies dead
hewn down in battle.   Mine is the greatest grief
he was both my kinsman   and my lord.'

Then he advanced   intent on battle
pierced one   with spear-point
seaman in that host   so that he lay on earth
killed with his weapon.   His comrades began to urge
friends and comrades   to press to the battle-front.
Offa spoke   shook his ash-spear
'What, so! Ælfwine has   urged you all
liegemen for our good   now our lord lies
earl on earth.   It is for the good of us all
that we   encourage each other
warriors to battle   that while we might
have and hold weapons   hard sword
spear and trusty sword.   Godric
Oddan's cowardly son   has betrayed us all.

When he rode away   on proud horse
very many men   thought it was our lord
so here on the field   folk were divided
shield-wall broken.   Curse him for behaving so
that he here put   so many men to flight!'

Leofsunu spoke   and raised his linden-shield aloft
defence-shield   answered the warrior
'I vow that I   will not move
a foot-step from here   but will advance
to avenge in battle   my lord and friend.
Nor around Sturmere   steadfast heroes need
reproach me that   my friend fallen
I lordless   journeyed homeward
went from battle   but weapon must take me
spear and iron blade.'   Wrathful he advanced
stoutly fought   scorned flight.
Dunnere then spoke   he shook his spear
a humble yeoman   called out over all
bade each warrior   avenge Byrhtnoth.
'None can flinch   who intends to avenge
lord in battle   nor care for life.'
Then they advanced   cared nothing for life
warriors began   to fight fiercely
fierce spear-bearers   and prayed God
that they might   avenge their lord
and on their enemies   inflict death.
The hostage began   eagerly to help
he was fierce kin   of the Northumbrians
Ecglaf's son   his name was Æscferth.
He did not flinch   in the fight
but rapidly shot arrows
sometimes pierced shield   sometimes tore warrior to pieces
ever and anon   inflicted some wound

for as long as he might   wield weapons.
Still Eadweard the long   stood at the forefront
ready and eager   spoke boasting words
that he would not flee   a foot-space of ground
give way   since his lord lay slain.
He broke the shieldwall   and with the warriors fought
until his giver-of-treasure   was worthily avenged
on those seamen   before he lay among the slain.
So did Æferic   noble comrade
eager to press on   fought resolutely.
Sibyrht's brother   and very many another
cleaved shield.   Valiant were they.
Shield-rim burst   and corslet sang out
terrible songs.   Then in battle Offa
struck the seafarer   that he fell to earth
and there Gadd's kinsman   sought ground.
Soon in battle   was Offa hewn down.
He had however achieved   what he'd vowed
before to his lord   to his ring-giver
that they should both   ride into the burgh
home safe and sound   or perish here
on the battlefield   die of wounds.
Befittingly he lay   slain near his lord.
Then was clash of shields.   Vikings advanced
enraged in battle   spear pierced often
doomed life-house.   Onward pressed Wistan
Thurstan's son fought   against those warriors.
He was in the throng   slayer of three
before Wigeline's son   lay among the slain.
There was hard conflict   warriors in battle
stood fast   warriors perished
weary of wounds.   The slain fell to earth.
Oswold and Eadwold   all the while
both brothers   exhorted warriors

their beloved kinsmen   words bade
that they there at need   should hold out
without weakening   use weapons.
Byrhtwold made a speech   shield raised aloft
(he was an old retainer)   brandished ash-spear
he very boldly   instructed warriors.
'Courage must be the fiercer   heart the keener
pride the greater   as our strength lessens.
Here our lord lies slain   noble all hewn
down in the dust.   Forever may he mourn
who now thinks to   turn from this fight.
I am old   I will not away
but think to lie slain   beside my lord
by so dear a man.'

So Æthelgare's son   emboldened them all
Godric to battle.   Often he sent spear speeding forth
deadly spear flew   among the Vikings
so he amid the host   stood foremost
cut down and harmed   until he fell in battle.
He was not the Godric   who fled the fight.

LAERTES

At times, now more and more with age,
as the ice-cap shrinks and the seas rise,
I feel unsustainable, as if on the verge
of extinction myself, behind my eyes.

The day swims in and out of light.
My head swims too. The earth is dry.
I struggle up and down my plot
carrying water for my husbandry.

My son came back alive. Though battles rage,
no reason now for me to dwell on wars
and casualties. I have enough scars
besides and wounds to nurse that come with age.

Vain to think I'll head for cooler latitudes
where the seasons still hold to their round,
somewhere the migrant birds have found
that suits the timing of their brief aubades.

No, I'll hold out here, while will-power lasts,
quietly resigned within my shrinking orbit,
as if that fabled country for old men exists
beyond regret and I have discovered it.

THE WILD BOY

John Francis Smith, Conwy 1965

The sea hurtles hard on a mounting gale.
Half-dead in his bunk below, he rubs
his eyes, struggling to wake and rise,
in the vast small hours. Sea air sharp as ice
flails in wait on deck, to cut free
last strands of sleep and send them flying
in her wake, among the ghosting gulls –
as the net hauls, and they gut fish,
counting the cost of bad luck, of torn gear
and catches lost; fuel-gauge wagging
a warning finger, veering to E for empty.

Call it a night, it says, and head for home,
out of the real world, into the lost,
where fortune and misfortune struggle
to balance books, to count the cost –
the value of what she'll land, rock-bottom,
their take-home pay a pauper's pittance.
You'd do as well to draw the dole
or chance your hand at the bookie's.
Yet veterans who've seen men perish
in the waste of waters and bold youths alike
look for the quick turn-around,
hooked on hope for a bumper catch
and come what may, the way of life itself.

The god that tames them must first tame the sea,
the deep ravines and plunging avalanches.
At which the wild boy says 'I'll take my chances.'
Who's hardly slept, so as not to be late,
and is now early, for his next trip,
waiting by the lobster-pot stack at 4 a.m.
This one I knew, a sometime schoolmate,
who sat out assembly with the Catholic
boys; as I did, but as a budding *refusenik*.

O ploughing and harrowing! O wake of gulls!
born with fish-bones in their throats,
to make them wail and yelp, to the end of time –
blood on their beaks, a primitive appetite
like his own to be free, to be an adult,
a skipper one day of the blue *Glendower*.

What else does he want from this risking,
from these wrecks of sea and sky? To have
his dumb need met this side of words

by reeling seas and wheeling birds,
fish spilling aboard, gaping and staring;
the beauty of fishing boats themselves,
their names, their colours and kinds –
all life cut away, to this necessity,
in the sea's high shadow and its tragedy,
its dawnlit idylls, its days and nights of storm.

What else is there to say? I waited for them,
under the last stars of the morning,
on a holiday errand for Arundell's
the fishmonger, to pick up a box or two
of plaice and whatever else might do.
In they came, pitching and rolling,
Betelgeuse and Venus, port and starboard,
and a riding light for the North Star fading –
as if still far out beyond the horizon,
not as they were, betwixt and between.
I caught his eye as he threw the line
but he looked straight through me
as they made her fast and swung the catch ashore
as if I had no business to be there.

THE AGE OF IRRELEVANCE

The poet steps into the plaza and begins
talking to himself. Might as well be Latin
or Greek to the generals at their caviar
and cocktails, bankers on their closing spree,
high summer evening cooling its late light
in the Lethe of the undiluted Thames,
Spenser in ruins, the Dean in his shroud,
Justice with a thumb in the scales. He says

the Age of Irrelevance lies in wait for all.
Too late for him anyway. His style's *de trop*.
Not even a warm-up act or sideshow
tugging at nostalgia's sleeve, to make some
rueful Oxbridge graduate remember
salad days and higher aspirations than
24/7 Commerce and Law, and this: cacophony
of liquidity, waitresses balancing trays
all the way from Belgrade, office romances,
texts, tweets, calls, nods, winks, conspiracies,
bonuses, high-tide traffic booming at their backs.
The market's free *ergo* take liberties. What
can't money buy? Whatever money is.
When was it not like this? (I'd like to know.)
See, they hardly notice he's there, muttering,
counting out his wealth on five digits – still
deluded that, if time's money, he invested well.

SPLICING

I watched him deftly join two ropes
with practised thumbs and fingers.
'Stronger than a knot,' he said, 'and
permanent.' The stone floor
barely lit by the open back door,
while the front rattled on its latch
against the gales that kept him land-bound,
working away at his latest repairs,
knowing he had more in the making
out there and nothing to be done
once the wind fell and the swell subsided
but count the damage.

DEATH BY WATER

When did you last see a dead bird? –
I rule out road-kill on tarmac –
their vanishing acts immaculate
in hedge-bottom, on wood-floor,
on mountainside, on moor…
but not here in the tidemark.

MAKING READY

I took the air along the quay
remembering every step of the way:
son et lumière in wheelhousing –
shadow-play making ready –
hearing on the cold sea air
engine-idling, in the dark,
pump spluttering bilge-water
feeling its age like an old man
as he pees against the wall –
a dinghy somewhere, outboard purring,
on out of hearing; a ghosting gull,
and then the voices.
'What's the worst injury you've seen?'
'Death,' said the trawlerman,
his eye gleaming. 'Death…'

DANCING DAYS FOR FISHING

She holds nothing steady on land or sea today.
But what-ho! proclaims, *What-ho!* her name.
Her compass needle dances a delicate ballet
pirouetting *en pointe*. 'Where, where, where…'
the gowned waves chorus.

Gulls in mobs clamour in the gods.
The mountains pitch and roll
like whales breaching among clouds
and the island at its mooring
spouts and spouts again all morning.

She parts the seas, thumbing through
for half-remembered lines,
myopic as late mackerel blinded by the light –
as jigging in mid-air they used to come
when she could count herself so lucky

that she could catch a hundred… and a tilly hand
that she could see so many all at once
to string through the gills
a youth's share, as nevermore
to hang on a handlebar for an encore.

NOTE: *Mackerel times-table*
3 mackerel = one hand
40 hands = one hundred (120)
to each 'hundred' add a 'tilly hand' for good luck or measure
1 mackerel = one poem

POEM AT 70

Let things lie as they fall.
The voracious day, the creaking night's
candelabra still lit up at the ball
in the caretaker's big house
where there's dancing every night, as I recall.

Gale-rip and rap of hail rattle my window
still at lights-out on that far coast.
Beachcomb there I say, as you hit the pillow.
See what spirits there are and laughter
in sea-shrubberies. Then sleep fast.

That's my advice. Better than
night-cap with stiffener or mogadon
for seeing clear the happy ghosts.
Not that I don't recommend a tipple
to keep the Adam's apple supple

with truth from the genie's bottle –
heading out to sea, as I like best,
night or day, repeating as I go:
as you reap so must you sow
and the half-said thing is dearest.

RIDDLE

I am the crescent moon fallen from the sky,
sharp as flint to touch and eye.

Before the foiled invasions of the sea
I flash and sing by night and day.

I rhyme with what is here to see.
Tell me what I am.

HILARY CHANDLER I.M.

I keep his compass on my desk
that it might guide me home.

A gift his widow gave me with
his hand-drawn charts of wrecks.

Hotspots to fish; and a mackerel line
on a bleached wooden frame

with a lead-weight cone to plumb
memory's sea-green currents

for shoals that once ran deep and wide.
Now mere spectres in the eighth sea.

I say 'home' but where might that be?
Where there's no epitaph: 'Lost at Sea'.

CRYING FOR THE WILDERNESS

He didn't belong there.
He was always going
to head elsewhere.
He looked around:
subject and object
but no grammar
to bring them together.
No common language
for bandage,
no common cause
still less applause

but gave him pause
everywhere he turned
in the human tide.
Not choice either
or prig's verdict
but it seemed of nature.
No, don't call it provincial
or sick for home.
Even the beauty
of river and tideway
of park and gallery
garden and palace
the *après midi* of a poem
bookshop and café
restaurant upon
restaurant – even
such delights
as returned his gaze
to its anonymity
the city's greatest gift –
fell by the wayside
of his madness
and left him crying
for the wilderness.

MEMORANDUM TO MACNEICE

Should I say I saw you in a vision? –
glimpsed your shade in my rear-view mirror,
my head cocked, like a budgerigar,
as I drove in your far-near country:
McNeillie calling MacNeice… MacNeice
are you there, still travelling

the fuchsia'd roads from Cleggan to Clifden
by Omey and through Claddaghduff... ?

While history, the morning after,
the night before, weather reeling in the sea's shadow –
its eyes turned down upon now
and nothing as lasting as bronze,
repeats itself again as farce,
a throwaway on Twitter's perch,
a thing of little consequence
quaint as thought or going to Church.

We are the ghosts in the machine
(and scarce your shadow cast at noon),
how right you were. Yet premature:
Rome's immortal story
still goes hurtling on, to ever greater ruin.
We are defined by differences
and our doom is bottomless
is all we know and all we need to know.

The train was ever off the rails
rattling through galaxies of inert stars,
the strings false, all along.
And so you sang and whistled in the dark
and so I hear you as I go
west in Eden on a day in June
the perch still burning,
and budgie in full song.

SPARROW-HAWK

I fatten her prey at the bird-table.
Does she think there's love between us?
Her billet-doux a patch of feathers,
a smudge of blood, a lower mandible,
once a single leg, the foot and claws,
enough for me to guess the species.

I sometimes know she's near
by the way the starlings scatter
in a sudden squall of wings
or the blackbird's dash for cover.
I've seen her on quiet evenings
perch unblinking on the bird bath

staring at me, as she digests her kill
her look so intense you might well
think we had a thing going –
perhaps from a former life –
more substantial than the air
on which suddenly she takes wing.

THE POET IN OLD AGE

No longer putting pen to paper –
seeing the world as if through glass
his gaze shadowed by his past
and little triumphs lost forever
his poems like distant islands
abandoned by their populations.
Yet the sea still knocking at his door.

MAKING ENDS MEET

Since you ask, I think of a door into the light,
light enough to make me blink and rub
the sleep from my eyes. Limestone light
backlit by sea. Light like a shadow
falling outside-in, on a stone floor.
And a kettle rattling to life loud as shingle,
its breath billowing like my own
as I lean there in the jamb, sipping hot tea,
savouring sea-light –
in those days when the island still
worked for a living, at sea or ashore,
or caught the boat for nevermore…
The tide out below. And the early worm
already turning in a bird's gut
like the one thought in my head
of lines to set and bait to put
a poem on my plate by evening.
Do I miss it? I have to own up, I do.
Though I have the best of it wherever I go
and the rest of it is everywhere still
struggling to make ends meet.

MEANWHILE (NEW POEMS)

'Always waiting, and what to do or say in the meantime
I don't know, and who wants poets at all in lean years?'
Hölderlin, 'Bread and Wine'

> *today's wisdom*
> *is tomorrow's error.*
> Andrew McNeillie

NOWHERE

And where will you go today, I asked myself.
'I've Nowhere in mind,' I said, and set off.

SIGN HERE

This is how it happens. The river
pours it into the harbour, out of
the far night inland, its pulse steady.
It will be ferried over on the tide
high at the pier-head now
straining at hawser and cable to be off.
I'm about to leave with it in my keeping.

I am coming back again, believe me,
I mean to. My heart behind it all
beats through the deep bay's litter.
The engine room sweats with oil and gleams
at its square of moon-marbling and shadow.
Take comfort as you hear its din going
up and down the iron ladder.

It isn't light. The moon has gone. The wind
blows from somewhere men are
harvesting in the fields by the graveyard.
There will be light to lead them soon.
I am bringing it in my wake by poem.
Never set sail without it says the bill of lading.
Now sign here on the dotted line.

WARM-UP ACT

The morning insists my coffee's getting cold.
It's early and frost still crisps the lawn.

Not everyone shall live until they're old
and some might rue the day that they were born.

There was a time I'd watch the dawn like this
and smoke the day's first cigarette.

Now caffeine is the poor alternative. Tant pis…
What is this life without regret?

Or procrastination's melancholy?
The aura of something that seems to be in code.

Not stubborn news, collective guilt,
beyond capture or redress in endless overload.

So I draw out my little warm-up act, and sip,
staring like an old man who's half out of it.

Rehearsing how to give the hour the slip.
Waiting for a cue to make an exit.

A TRIAL SEPARATION

Dear reader, I leave you
to my own devices
as you never left me
but peered over my shoulder
at my every move
to escape your jurisdiction
invigilating my vigilance.

Noting how I cover my page
with my forearm
like a shifty schoolboy –
but tell me why?
I've never looked to give you
what you want.
You don't set the questions.

Yet there you are.
What is wrong with you?
I see no point in
a trial separation, thank you.
Get it into your head.
I don't want to see you
or hear from you again.

It ought to be against the law.
Or must I forever keep watch,
listening out for the dog
in the yard to bark
at the slightest hint of you
coming up behind me
stalking in the dark?

THEN V. NOW

Then holds its ground, though its hour's gone.
At least it had days once, while now has none.

Now is all talk – birdsong, May-fly, blossom,
beauty, billing, cooing, heaving bosom…

Now is the news going twenty-four-seven.
But it's all as nothing without a then.

Then what, you ask, more of the same?
Then the evidence and the blame.

AS

As on the night before a new adventure
when what you've planned might not become the future
and sleep's as broken as a choppy sea
and waiting makes the clock crawl round
slower than Zeno's progress to infinity,
its hands going down and up again.
As reports come in that a father and son
are missing presumed drowned,
and all sailings are cancelled until further notice.

(As when you open in parenthesis,
as if what's to come might ever end
and be lifted away, or framed like a picture,
summed up by a title and a *fecit* signature.)
As you consider your options, and resort to plan-B,
as the couple cancel their honeymoon,
as the daughter from Rhode Island

having just missed her mother's funeral
finds herself grieving between the meanings of terminal.

As you sit elbows-on-knees staring at your feet,
waiting and staring for as long as forever
or pace up and down, trying to make sense
of what's happening, with one eye on the weather
and an ear to what they're saying about
the prognosis and the latest turn of events,
as one damned thing leads to another
and nothing changes or even relents –
why not consider the lilies of the field for once?

Think what it means to have time on your hands,
time if not space to dwell, to see
what it means, simply to be
at the beck of no one's commands,
to be stuck ashore, yet all at sea.
Didn't you always want to break free?
Haven't we all heard you cry 'If only…'
Well, now's the time to give only a try,
because only is here and feeling lonely.

AFTER TIM ROBINSON'S TIME IN SPACE

i.m. Máiréad

After the obituaries, the *éloges* and sail-shaped remembrances.
After the crowds have left on the boat
and the pollution of their footfall dies away with the evening.
After autumn's equinox begins the purer dream of winter –
that's when to settle in to work and when I've thought of you
most often, in the capital of monochrome, at Fearann an Choirce,
in your storm-walled house with its empty window-frame,
                                        overlooking the west.
And after all now, I find myself
thinking of you all the time – bald, and silent as a Buddha
as you've become, staring from a photo on my wall,
from the night we first met, as we'll never meet again,
to enjoy our squawks, in honour of the *sgarbh* and the Rock.
The last wise man gone, another ghost in the ranks up there,
gathered with Thoreau and Melville, to watch below
worst fears for Earth and humankind come true
in our wireless shapeless world, bound by the heptagonal sea,
as the covid strikes us down, as, bitter irony of ironies,
it struck you; and puts us in our place as we deserve,
to rethink our time in space, and dwell on who knows what to come?

THE GOOD SHIP

Never rename a vessel
but leave memory to trawl
in her wake. Tragedy
furrows the seas. Weather
holds true to its lunacy.
Boats founder. Souls grieve.

While she changes
by repair as she ages:
a heart transplant in
the engine department,
new winch-gear and sonar –
to say nothing of you.

Know her by name.
Feel the ballast there
as she soars and plunges
to the grounds that are
the grounds of her being.
Know her through time.

Call to her as she is now
and as you remember her
who caught your heart
long ago. And see her home
as you used to when
you were both young.

from THE SHELL GUIDE TO NOWHERE

Out here along the sea's ragged margin
where villages die out by the hour, as places
on the hill stand to fall emptied of hope
and all promise of a come-back by
returning prodigals, looking to see their
last years out where they were born,
who don't make it, who die wherever
they washed up, their truths unknown
by those they knew. Out here, you'll find
few visitors, even in the summer season,

so far from the nearest B&B, but it's worth
a few minutes of your time, to stop
and take a look around at history's latest
among the detritus of internal combustion,
where the one-eyed petrol pump,
like a modernist clock of early 1950s vintage,
with a finger in its ear, outstares all,
in a retrospective shared by
oil drums, a heap of tyres, an old bus
on pillars of bricks, a fishing boat sinking
in a little field, random scrap, gas-cylinders,
welding gear in an abandoned workshop,
the usual masterpieces and poor turn-out
by the locals, who mostly keep indoors
with their ailments and quiz shows,
and not only during the winter months.

BOOKMARK

When I opened the door and looked,
there was no one there, not a soul.
It was only the weather announcing itself.
I greeted it and it came in. The roof
and the empty loft welcomed it and
the fire took a deep breath and exhaled
the day's first smoke up its brow
beyond the mantelpiece. Come in and
sit down, I said. I'm just finishing my
porridge. I won't be long but it was
impatient and told me to hurry up
and hovered, half-in half-out, on the step.

I heard the slow downhill clop of a horse
telling me my neighbours were already
on their way, soon to break into a trot
after McDonough's corner, where
the fuchsia used to bleed all summer long
under the high Atlantic sky and low mists.
The pages of my book on the table
fluttered so that I lost my place,
reading out of the corner of my eye
as I raised the spoon to my mouth.
Though I can still remember where I was
even from as far away as here.

THE FERRYMAN

How would it be, do you think?
There would be mist, I'd say,
shielding the shore, first forward
then aft, as if to ease you
between being alive and being
dead; if there is death there
and not just after-life, as I've heard
is what's in store with Dido
and that crowd Aeneas saw
or Aengus as they call him here.

The sea would be a millpond
I suppose and the light ghostly.
I've made such crossings before
and on a one-way ticket too
in which Bartley Beatty made
a little tear as I stepped aboard
nodding and asking how things were.

Not bad, considering, I might say
after a lock-in at the Castle
just a short step from the quay

where one evening Anthony
Hernon missed his step between
the boat and the wall
and so jumped his turn
for the sea-road home.
There were so many Bartley thought
he had a job for life
after serving his time
on the platform of a London bus
as if he'd been invented by Louis MacNeice.

But they laid him off.
To make ends meet he drove
a taxi in Galway, ferrying drunks
out into the sticks
to far-flung bungalows down
fuschiad lanes by little loughs
in barren bogs, places so remote
they could have been
on the far shore of the Styx
for all you might know.

SALVAGE

Take what you will aboard *SS Memory*
made fast to the harbour-wall.

There are things to come you'll never see.
No truth's more universal.

Meanwhile keep setting sail
and hope what will be won't be.

WINNOWING AT CILL MHUIRBHIGH HARBOUR

August 1969

It was an August evening.
The tall rye had fallen
to the sickle, as if so long ago
Virgil saw it happen

or one of those old prophets
in the Bible. The sea had risen
in the horseshoe bay. You
could feel it chill the air

as it came, to flail against
the harbour wall. Its grain
ribbed, silver as the crescent moon.
The flailing done now

I watched him winnow
as the small breeze blew
and the chaff fell to gather
at the high-water line

of his year, the grain
pattering like rain on
a sheet of tarpaulin,
as if it were spring and his seed sown.

While up in the North
an ill wind blew South.
And winter came to stay
as if it would never go away.

BREAKWATER (CONTRA PLATO)

Here, far inland as I am,
where the seven-sided clouds blow by
and the gulls that follow the garbage dozer
proclaim their origin behind the trawler –
I take my stand, in this waste of words
holding my ground, as fate pounds
and sluices through me, by storm,
by flood, by metaphor in
a wake of pages, telling
of grief and joy, tragedy and miracle:
tales that embroil and spellbind
between worlds – as the sea stands
and falls, falls and stands, eternally
against all that asserts authority
and distrust of poets and poetry.

SLIPWAY

You can tell they're out there somewhere
because she's not here.
But you wouldn't know otherwise.

Unless from this fresh keel-scrape
that will fade like a fish out of water
when the tide brings them back.

FEEDING HABITS

Their weather-eyed magnetic clocks,
their bird-table timetables, their
GPS travels above the house
to field or water, wood or rock,
moorland, mountain, island –
light-metred, almost to the minute;
their long migrations North and South:
feed my habit and dependence on them,
as they come and go, to find food,
to sing their songs, to breed –
and feed my weather-eye, hallowing
the moment, and harrowing me
with remembrance and hope,
however much time begs to differ
and winds the year until
its spring comes close to breaking.

BEYOND GOOGLE

Only with a boat to catch might I go
by the high road, if time was tight, and the ferry
strained at the quay and the timetable,
and the skipper glanced between his watch
and the last of us, as we came down
scurrying and struggling, though we knew
she wouldn't leave as long as there were
any to be seen. Stragglers out of sight
were out of mind, after all, and couldn't
complain. Were their hearts really in it?
There were such laid-back days once,
when it didn't greatly matter; and some

would glance at the clock and shrug
and take their chance next time,
not linger so long at their glass and talk,
the weather of their minds permitting –
to have a change of scene, where they
weren't much known, if known at all.

A person was wealthy in that way then
with what he stood up in, and enough
to get by, between one hour and another,
on the island or ashore, out of season.
Such lives there were, off the radar,
unless some incident occurred,
a fracas, an ill-judged step at the harbour,
briefly brought to light in magistrate's
verdict or coroner's report, recorded in
a corner of the *Tribune*. Even so
it wasn't going to travel far, or last long.
Enter any of it in your search engine
and, I promise, you'll be gone a long time,
way beyond the rim of memory.
So long that no one will remember you
or know what you're talking about,
if you ever make it back with an answer.

THE DISTANT COUSIN

I don't have their language
though their look's
stamped over me
like a smudged postmark
on an envelope from a foreign place.

Or welcome on a doormat
worn to a shadow. Why
do I feel guilt
when they don't? – first on their list
to call to the funeral.

AUNT EDITH

And if I could make sense of it, what would that be?
To make sense, or to say, it doesn't make sense.
Who is she to you? I remember the woman asking,
a question to my question. And when I said
I was part McGarva, part McNeillie, she said
oh *those* McNeillies as if we had a reputation
I didn't know about and pointed down the road
to where Aunt Edith lived in the tidy house with
a clock and a cat, lace doilies, and photographs
of a brother or was it her father, out in Ceylon
in the long-ago of empire. He was one of us
anyway, but not really, not one of me.
How few of those there seem to be about.
I suppose I know two, or even three, unevenly.
And between us we don't make a lot of sense.

A FIRST GOODBYE

Walk the town by its back-streets to the sea,
with their sudden sights of promised liberty
where none exists, although you sail away
and wave a first goodbye, but of how many?

Is this the lesson you left to learn,
if not the one you had in mind
and might have learnt just as well,
better and worse, if you'd stayed behind?

THE ROAD TO NOWHERE

Scrape the stars off night's windscreen
and drive to arrive when you can.

Wipers labouring, heater broken,
breath condensing... Through the snow's

inferno where the blizzard blows
in the headlights' funnel. Steady now.

Easy with the brakes... Keep the show
on the road. Whatever you do, arrive.

And never try to turn back: get there alive.
No matter you won't know if you don't.

EXILE'S LAMENT

You can travel back to where you came from.
But be sure to think about it. What
was on your right hand will now be
on your left. What zigzagged down
the valley's course, will zag and zig
the other way, and everything you see
enjoy a different aspect to the light.
Take note of this and think on.

The river flows against you that
ran with you then, eager to lure you
over the border and away. Now
it helter-skelters off behind you;
and, if not dead and gone, those
you knew will all be changed from
when you upped and left them
and not know you from Adam.

Though some might know your name.
Anyone will tell you, the tale's
as old as time. But don't be fooled,
time's of the hour, and so are you.
Better to take a look around,
then go by the way you came
zigzagging with the river until
you're back to where you don't come from.

LIKE GOLDFINCHES

This late spring, and spring was late,
the Goldfinches came
riding in the tops of next-door's silver birch
as it took on a wash of green.
I thought they'd soon move on
after the cold snap and the sunflower hearts
back into the country, and
they seemed to vanish, soon enough.
But I was wrong.

As this morning I see, all cover blown,
half-way into June, their fledglings come
sipping at the garden pond
down among the 'Wild Iris' – dipping,
flitting, twittering, here and there,
and now, and then, toppling about,
like fallen trapeze artists, to bounce
up and down and spring, wobbling
to their feet on the anti-heron net.

Then in fright at something
or nothing mirrored in the pond,
up they whirr away, into
the tops of next-door's silver birch
to bring a circle round and be
like Goldfinches, windblown –
first-generation suburbanites though they are,
lost thistle-seed tweakers –
delicate picklocks at the feeder,
condemned to join me here,
serving life as I am.

BEACHCOMBING

This is the place to come for it:
this narrow strand in your mind
where the waves comb and stumble
and the tide heaves, birthing
and memory's keel crushes the shingle
with a delicious sound.

And the sea scribbles
in bladderwrack-black-ink as I do:
I WAS HERE and again
HERE further up or down the coral sand.
As if aiming at an ideal it can't locate
no matter how often it tries.

Narrowing its eye (it only has the one)
to see how its handiwork looks
from low tide and how
it might be improved: by some neap readjustment
of sandgrains on a fly-paper
ribbon of wrack.

Or by the precise placing of an orange marker buoy
newly brought to light,
the remains of a cormorant…
Until it loses patience with itself
and turns the ocean inside out,
dumping more wonders ashore.

This is beachcombing's lasting lure:
that you can't guess what
treasures will catch your eye
among the plastic debris
as you lose yourself in the sharp light
of the ozone sound-warp

relishing Thalassa's folly
that she cannot walk away
but must try again:
with the bloated carcase of a seal,
the egg-case of a dogfish…
not knowing where to draw the line.

THREE SONNETS

1 A HAMES

How I wanted to be them, to drive
nature in with a pitchfork. For the rope
not to cut my palms. (O slender hope.)
For the horse to know me and forgive
my want of horse sense, not lead me but be led,
not show me up before them; and not
for Tom to say, 'Don't be making a hames of it' –
the way I forked the rye-straw overhead
so that it fell and slithered down the other side.
How kind they were, and how they knew
what it meant to me, if not where it would lead,
no more than I, still trying as I am to know
just why, leading or led, I labour here
at this – making a hames of it again, I fear.

'to make a hames' – an Irish expression, to make a mess of
    something; to put the hames upside down on a horse's collar.

2 PHOTOGRAPHIC EVIDENCE

Field-labour may be a thing of long ago
but to me it seems more like yesterday.
I can vouch for it. I have photos too,
if not the holiday callouses still. Maybe a far-away
look, though – like those caught in their eyes,
in the wink of a shutter, taken from time.
And as suddenly returned, to step from
the frame and reclaim their identities.

I can name them across three generations
in the photographic age. I even knew
the later ones and their passions.
I've written down their details, as if I know
what it is to remember. O tender care
for those who aren't here and weren't there.

3 LIKE CLOCKWORK

Time ticks louder and fainter, as round
the dark corn and round again a machine
makes short work of the hard-worked land,
headlights glaring at a harvest moon
and dew falling, into the early hours,
tomorrow, they warn, turning to rain.
And still like clockwork, autumn stirs
in the early North; the goose skein
sharpens its arrow and tunes its voice
for the raid South – all by memory,
magnetic mystery, cold and light, not choice –
gabbing and gaggling in the steep sky,
programmed to arrive as harvest's done,
heralding winter as it's still known.

THE CORNCRAKE TIMER

crex crex crex crex crex crex crex crex crex crex crex crex crex crex crex
crex crex crex crex crex crex crex crex crex crex crex crex crex crex
crex crex crex crex crex crex crex crex crex crex crex crex crex
crex crex crex crex crex crex crex crex crex crex crex crex
crex crex crex crex crex crex crex crex crex crex crex
crex crex crex crex crex crex crex crex crex crex
crex crex crex crex crex crex crex crex crex
crex crex crex crex crex crex crex crex
crex crex crex crex crex crex crex
crex crex crex crex crex crex
crex crex crex crex crex
crex crex crex crex
crex crex crex
crex crex
crex
cre
x
   c   r
     x   e
  c   r
     e
 r   x
    c
      r
  e   e
    x   c
 x   c   r
      r e
c   x e
  r   x
x c   x   e
c r e   r e   x   c re x   crex

MEANWHILE

Now, don't roll your eyes when I say
it wasn't always so. That meanwhile
once went starved of news, subsisting
on thin air and memories. It prayed.
It thought of you more than you could know.
It lay awake listening to the gale
and what the shipping forecast had to say.
It read your letter over and over
and went about taking the chill off your room,
with the gas fire and the Calor cylinder;
aired bed-linen, fussed and cleaned.
It lamented the squalling rain at the window
and stared minutes on end into the grey
where spume and rain dashed together
along the cliffs, the sea's first obstacle
between here and America.
It remembered the day you left and
wondered where you are now. And
knew too well how long it was
since your last visit. It took its time
and busied itself to make time fly.
Until at last the postmistress came over
with the message you were aiming for
the longer B-sailing on Thursday.

THE NEW BOAT

Slim and unstable as a Connemara
in its teens jumping at the slightest
skittish wave, as if a grasshopper
gave it a scare by the road. So

on a windborne day she rolls and
pitches, and bridles sidling –
and won't be fooled when
they rein her in at the end
and coax her towards harbour
but bucks and rears kicking
in the last of the Sound's pull
towards farther and greener idylls.

THE NORTH STAR

The harbour light lowered and lifted –
a canary in a mine-shaft fluttering
guttering but unquenched. Lead kindly
as she wrangles and haggles for passage
through wheeling collisions of light
flashed at death's threshold, hell's mouth,
heaven's gaping gate, the narrow strait
and close scrape, Davy's Locker and lamp
together, rocky seamark and landmark
vying on a soul's darkest before the dawn,
gull and gale crying until depth do us part –
glass-eyed cod, haddock, monk, on ice –
the crew, lids propped, dying to turn in,
to drown in sleep until they wake
restless to put out again as much for
the sake of it as for pay's lean packet.

THE *NAOMH ÉANNA*'S LAST VOYAGE

for Michael Muldoon

Who saw her leave, who watched her
turn south that time and wondered
had she lost her mind, her bearings...
her skipper shipwrecked
when something in him hit a rock?
And left him crying: 'It's all too much.
A sailings, B sailings... standing off
for the folk to row their emigrants out,
towing their cattle and horses,
as if we were on the South Seas
only paying our way with letters and groceries,
Guinness canisters, bottled gas – un-
stable, labouring in hard weather,
many a miracle she never capsized...'

Who saw her go? running for her life,
using those white ships from Japan
for cover, the tuna longliners, bound
for the ends of the Earth beyond.
And who didn't? by every tide, and every
sailing since, coming home or leaving,
on her turbo-charged replacements.

SONG

i.m. Myles Joyce and Iain Munro

On a long night in the pub
when the sea ran fast in the Sound,
I sat with Myles who was drunk
but sang as well as he could
and held his arms out to sing
while one either side took a hand
to pump it out of him.

Over he sang and again
and up and down they pumped
as if to keep us afloat in the drink
that seized us in its swell
as the song rose and fell.
And what he sang was grief
and of his own survival.

'Three days and nights,' he sang,
'three days and nights adrift
with a dead man before
we were washed up ashore
on the coast of Clare.'
All of fifty years ago
when I was young, you know?

Little did I think then
I'd have such a song of my own one day
and feel his grief again
year in year out come May
and learn the hard way that
what never can be mended
will ever have its say.

MISSING THE BOAT

So much, he spent his afternoons,
like a widower, on his own,
parked up in the high lay-by,
window down, scanning the ocean
with his binoculars, feeling his loss
all the way – as he had in his youth
the day she wouldn't wait
a moment longer for him
and he ran down the quay waving,
calling after her in vain.

LUCKY HORSESHOE

I once walked a crescent field by
a horseshoe bay, looking for a horseshoe
cast by a bay, somewhere
in the new spring grasses.

(I tell no lie.) He went in with four
and came out with three.
It could only be there
but it wouldn't be found.

For a while I suppose
it hung about, then went to ground
still waiting to make someone's luck
until too frail from rust

ever to hang on a door-nail
still less ring out on the road

to the ground-bass of the sea
with its windblown manes.

If I'd found it, might it be
lost to memory now and
forgetting prove to be
where true luck's made?

OWT OF THISE BLAKE WAWES...

after Chaucer 'Troilus and Criseyde' Book II, ll 1–7

To sail out of this black ink…
O wind! O wind! begin to blow
my pages clear. For right now
the good ship has such toil,
I can hardly steer her at all.
The sea's so tempestuous
I despair…
               But see, at last,
the first day of hope arrives
and I can take my story up again.

MEDITATIONS IN A BOATSHED

L
A
Y

H
E
R

K
E
E
L

F
R
O
M

S
T
E
M

T
O

S
T
E
R
N

FRAME HER LENGTH WITH
UPTURNED ARCHES TO
HER GUNWALE'S WIDTH
AT DEEP MIDSHIPS AND
PLANK HER RIBS
FROM FORE
TO AFT

There I was wandering, to pass
the hour, when I came across
a boatshed, in the hinterland
of Nowhere. I don't understand
how I got there. How I got here
still I wonder too. I'm not sure,
perhaps I'd had a few. But clear
as day, the door was open and
I poked my head inside to find
a man alone and hard at work,
deep within the shadowy dark,
toiling with steambox and iron,
warping and shaping his vision,
the first new order on his books
for months – and last, on most outlooks.
Some jump to blame the muse
when work dries up. A poor excuse
and no use to the like of him
for whom the muse is just a scam.
The bottom's out of the market
from Finisterre to Fastnet
from Stornoway to Nantucket
Baltimore to Ghazaouet.
The bottom's out of the planet
too, say those who know about it.

He didn't seem to notice me
though I was plain enough to see.
Perhaps I was seeing double,
my mind in a little trouble.
But no work of making welcomes
a spectator. It's true for poems
I know. Remember the reader,
the critic over your shoulder?
Then why not so for boats?
Don't both proceed by second thoughts?
One step forward, another back,
a slip, a fix, a different tack.
The surprises of invention
always will improve intention.
Back to the drawing board we go
to find out what we do not know.
Boat or poem it's all the same.
Both crafts demand a form of rhyme,
port to starboard every time.
So, work according to your will
and work, and work, and work until
your efforts find an even keel.

To take the breakers at a leap,
the leaper must be shipshape,
out where the land bucks on the waves
and nothing takes unless it gives.
Concentrate. Don't pause to wonder
what the future holds. The future
is as water. Match inner states
with outer. Leave fate to the Fates,
and Fortune to her own devices.
When was the world not in crisis?
Who doesn't know that doing

nothing, ends in being nothing?
Who isn't driven by a passion
should have stayed behind in Eden.
Know virtue is its own reward
and do your best to shape the word.
Remember Noah and his ark?
Now settle down to build your barque.
Weather life's storm. Heal your soul.
Wield adze and mallet, plane and awl,
and let the music in them sing.
Life is short and the craft long.
What is it worth without a song?
Fast forward is the world's way
but your watchword must be delay,
up to your knees in shavings and
sawdust. Work with, and without, end.

Come what may of what will come
love is the baby in the pram.
Don't throw her out with the sea-
water but sing her a lullaby.
Sing waly waly down the brae
and waly waly love be bonny
and other sleep-tight rhymes of old.
Heart's care the cargo in your hold.
The status quo's been overthrown.
The disaffected have spoken,
the neglected and downtrodden.
The seas have broken the sea wall.
There's chaos in the Capitol
as Rome takes yet another fall.
What can the individual do
against the mass? I'd like to know.
Wave from a far horizon

off the coast of oblivion
mouthing SOS and May Day?
What else might a soul do or say?
Seek sanctuary from the world
and respite in work's solitude
seems for now the sanest option
in face of 24/7 global opinion.
Refine your sense of proportion.

Don't let yourself be overawed.
Let labour be its own reward
as well, until the call to board.
Don't speculate about your purpose,
time enough to chart a course –
cry to heaven, 'Abandon Ship',
'Lower Away', though waves be steep,
join those in peril on the deep,
seeking refuge from disaster
somewhere not in the hereafter.
Let go fore and aft, and say farewell.
Follow the *Pequod* if you will
or play it safe along the coast
to put in somewhere in the past
where the drowned hurl against the rocks
in yarns of storms and tragic wrecks.
Or say good riddance to the last
of England at its very worst,
the dark side of its bill of lading
black as Ahab's soul out whaling,
a tale a million times as thick
as a million copies of *Moby-Dick*.
Put a good ship to good use
its good name still might come off worse:
the *Windrush* scandal a disgrace

as shocking as the Dreyfus case –
seen off with a resignation,
whitewash for a troubled nation.

Oh why not embark at last
and go barefoot before the past
first round one cape then another
shriven by the wildest weather?

But first attend to what's at hand,
get in the zone, embrace 'no-mind',
as in *Zen and the Art...* of anything
from archery to motor-cycling.
Study that plan of a ship's lifeboat,
a double-ender, clinker-built...
of the kind you once knew well
from youth's immortal idyll
following shoals of mackerel.
Long before you heard of Ishmael,
you knew you were a voyager –
long before you read Homer.
Before the seas ran threadbare or
the poet saw eternity
in a grain of plastic debris.
Just keep making your poem
to the very crack of doom
out here in this derelict waste,
landscape of a broken past –
a terminal's wrecked hinterland,
its map a mirror to your mind,
where time's washed up, and run aground.

A POSTCARD FROM THE TEMPLE

The news is of the hour and only paper thin.
Days tell you this every day. Pay them heed.
Count them if you wish. Cross them off the calendar
as it turns the four corners of the year.
Déjà-vu has no meaning in their world.
Learn to be like days. Autumn flails
and winnows all today. Clear your mind
of dead wood… all brittle thought.
Winter and the birds will come in greater number
with a sharper eye and hunger.
Snow will melt; or settle, joining earth to sky,
and the goldfish lie torpid, until spring
brings out its dead by crocus-light.

SINK OR SWIM

The sea's not entirely foreign:
we also never learn.

We too start out complete
and then repeat, repeat…

with variations on a theme
between sink or swim.

FOR THE TIME BEING

The island doesn't haunt me,
far from it. Nearer but still far
I haunt it. Then what passes

between us? The ferry out
never meets the ferry back.
No matter the tide-table
or weather conditions.
Log this for the time being.

SEA-BIRDS CROSSED THE LENS

I noted them by species.
They don't name themselves.
Nature has no nomenclature.
But they have forms, markings
that distinguish them,
languages, cries, call-notes,
behaviours that encode
their world, their purposes,
their exits and alarms. Cold
comfort is no concept in
their tongue, nor earthling.
They speak hunger and
the patois lust in spring.

I sat there forearms on knees,
to steady my binoculars,
hands clasped crudely at my temples,
as if in makeshift prayer,
wondering how much longer
I could keep my vigil up,
bearing witness on the cliff-top
above the dancing Atlantic.

And what for? What have I
concluded since, from my

observations, as the tide
mounted, and the gannets
went at it headlong, and the guillemots
floated their flotillas on
the swell among the rafts of weed,
and the waves broke
and lashed the rocks with spray,
light turned liquid,
booming and splattering,
the gulls arced and crossed,
the cormorants laboured
to be airborne, all in a sound-scape
as endless as the ocean
and its seven-sided shores?
O what have I ever learnt
but that a question beats
an answer every time?

THE ROCK

I'm walking out from home again,
from the backdoor step.
I'll be gone for a few hours and
it gives me a good feeling to set off.
But I might weary before I'm back
because it's a long footslog
all the way round the island.

One thing I notice apart from the sea
that's always at least one wave ahead
is the absence of clichés here
between the houses at least
with their B&B vacancies and

welcomes to the visitors
towards the close of the season.

Not to mention the Leprechaun houses.
Otherwise the place is pristine,
turned out to perfection by years
of experience and a sense of proportion
anyone would envy and wish
to be like in their minds
so often brought to breaking point.

Already some have their boats
hauled in and parked along
the side of the house and the pots
stacked and are thinking
of the holiday to Corsica or
even Rhode Island, in a good year,
to set their world in perspective.

I'll be leaving myself before long.
If my luck holds and I'm spared
I might come back, weather permitting,
to the Rock, the mothership
of my double life, my selves.
But for now, I am still here
and on the last step to the door.

ONE IN THE EYE

for David Jones, Maenan

I

When my mother's waters broke, I washed ashore
at Colwyn, a child of the Irish Sea.
The evening set away towards Glanmore.
My shipping forecast told another story:
from Great Orme's Head to Mull of Galloway;
our folk up there; and at Winmarleigh or
scattered all about, my mother's family.
Then blown to pieces by the Great War.

Here's the schoolroom and this is geography.
Here pinpointed there, between the physical
and political. Next it must be history
and something not quite metaphysical:
what became of a moment, in image
or word, for a future to assay the damage.

2

Now washed up here, unimaginably,
the very man himself, the slow achiever.
Child of another war, the latecomer,
absent by nature. The one that isn't me
and wasn't him. Though our name's ticked present
in the register and I can still prove
to Miss Lewis who's dead that we're alive
and haven't forgotten our punishment.

The eye is not the same as the mind –
the treasurer of memories that dun me
to pay interest on their debts. Sound-
tracks blow at the window. There the sea

hangs from its horizon like a canvas
rolled down for visitations like this.

3
Melancholy the ordnance survey of loss.
My eye traces there so I might climb
Llanelian hill again, towards a likeness
here – taken from the life, stolen from time
that's called at Y Ddraig Goch no more,
now someone's home or second home –
in a flood of sea-light, and the wind-farm
marking it on the spot, out on the moor:
cartwheels set in a gate, going nowhere,
or going at it with a will offshore
to save the planet. Half-schooled by rote
I used to say: the more things change, the more
they stay the same. Now Earth casts doubt,
adrift with neither cable nor anchor.

4
I can see it all from here. The vivid
nitrates in the little fields. Scarcity
of birds and fishless streams that boyhood
nightlined for his breakfast or for tea.
The reservoir, the Nature Trail, the Ruin
of Time… Called long ago on Joe Erskine,
on Brian London. Or some other hero
held in that age between ten and zero
in a boy's mind, live on the wireless, and
in the photos of *Boxing News*. 'Sugar Bag'
Robinson, a sugar bag on either hand,
asking his father how he'd like 'One in the eye,
like Bruce Woodcock, by me.' O little wag
at the wall counting out his do or die.

5
O hugger-mugger life, before the ref steps in,
or the corner men throw in the towel.
It has no likeness now. It isn't down
in any map but of the mind or soul,
a true place, and common to us all
wherever our mother's waters broke.
Time outside self-consciousness and clock
when all is done wide-eyed and full
of trust... Until the Age of Reason brings
Miss Lewis with her pounding fist and ruler.
And with her, her unsorry kind, their Songs
of Experience warning of foul weather
and worse to come, in the forecast of their
fallen hearts – of Innocence beyond repair.

NOT FOR SUPPER

    after Poetry for Supper *by R.S. Thomas*

I met him and his eye
cold as winter and quick
as Anafon in spring.
It was easy to avoid
the awkward subject.

We talked of trout
as they used to be
in the mountain streams.
Of Merlin, Pipit,
Cuckoo and Wheatear.

It was easy to discuss
the merits of the old patterns.
Coch-y-bonddhu,
Peter Ross, March Brown,
Hare's Ear Nymph.

To stare into the distance
and the silence
their names bequeathed us
was enough without once
mentioning it.

BLACK-HEADED GULLS, LLYN CONWY

What can I tell you to update you now?
If you ask me I'd say everything,
if everything were anything I know.
What invalidates memory? Nothing
I remember. Look, here I am again.
Nothing up my sleeve. No miracle
to pull out of a hat, a cloud to crown
the little island as they did that time
at the height of the nesting season
heckling and squalling in the rain
that kept the midges down
so we might fish on into the evening.

LLANELIAN

Do Sundays come here still, short of breath,
long on faith, loitering in the churchyard
after a service, as they used to, trying hard

to read the headstones through the rain? Death
in mothballs. Odour of yew, and naphalene
in the heart's tallboy. Or fire-and-brimstone
of the Word not made-to-measure, but one-
size-fits-all, in the Chapel, thanks to Calvin.
Is that faint whisper a choir giving voice
or just the wind passing through, as it goes
where it listeth? Are these parishioners' cars
outside the pub, the church's next-door neighbour,
busiest on the day of rest from labour?
Are prayers still said? I'd say they are.

WHERE ARE THE SOLDIERS?

for Elaine

At the window, Lough Swilly
silvers the morning, with a sharp line of light
down the shore, here in the Free State.
It is March, the month of patron Saints.
Over the hills and far away.

We talk about origins and names we share,
worlds in common; and their fate
to have lived through the Troubles,
mine to be born in Wales, by fortune's grace.
Over the hills and far away.

It was as if they'd never heard of it
or never thought it a serious place.
Until one piped up with a memory
from girlhood, at the age of eight –
Over the hills and far away.

On a visit to an aunt in Manchester,
they'd gone for a drive there.
'Now you're in Wales,' they told her,
'You've crossed the border.'
'But *where*,' she cried, in disbelief, '*where* are the soldiers?'

Over the hills and far away, they said.
Over the hills and far away...

THE SOCIAL CONTRACT

I saw it with my own eyes, and put it in my notebook.
Tabernacle Row on the slide, its gardens washed
away in the Amman. They would not forsake
home for safety, what home meant to the last,
what could not be recreated. Slag overhead
and Aberfan in recent memory, to be always so.
The slippery slope of neglect and unintended
consequence. The 'authorities' prone to let things go.
To cut corners. To meet targets. To be expedient.
I climbed down among the rocks to dramatise
the camera angle and wrote my story. It didn't
make the front page. It took no one by surprise.
Certainly not the wheezing young men
who struggled to make it to the Benefit Office
and struggled harder to make it back again.

BESIDE THE SEASIDE, BESIDE THE SEA

The pier clangs and booms, spills and hisses with spray,
limpet and barnacle bleach the tideswept pilings and girders.
Brine turns lips and tongues to salt. Empty deckchairs

fill their sails and scuttle down the planks. Over my shoulder in a splash
sudden heavyhearted rain killjoys the town again.

Souses the candy-floss bouffants. Puts a spike in umbrella sales.
Flutters the gulls on the tarmac's sudden mirror.
They have no vacation, only a vocation, to starve
the time god sent them, whatever godsend-sandwich
or bag of sodden chips windfalls their ravenous squalls.

The hotels discolour, their stucco tattered and gnawed.
'Vacancies' their windows declare. Vacancies here are everywhere.
Insatiable days pile up their big-bellied clouds.
Thin rain blows on ahead, looking for somewhere to dry out,
before the crowds descend. It's upside down this world of ours.

But here briefly downside up takes a turn at holiday,
time immemorial, beside the seaside, beside the sea.
See the furloughed stroll, their every move watched closely,
by empty rooms, and zero hours, and those gangs of gulls
yelping and keening at migrant winter in the wings.

ONE NIGHT ONLY, CRAIG-Y-DDERWEN RIVERSIDE HOTEL

Suddenly, staring at the river as it ran
inaudibly beyond the window, waiting
for my order of salmon *en croûte* to arrive,
I found myself upstream, stepping
like a ghost into Evans's hatchery,
with its ladder of tanks and filters
and stripped eggs and shoaling fry
bound for the sea one day, and the black rainfall
of the North rushing, loud as a waterfall,
about his laboratory or honey hive

on the valley-side above the Lledr.
A man on a mission to save the salmon,
no more his old self either, battered
near to the other side of hearing by
wild men poaching for the hotels.

THE GOOD BOOK

In all the acres of time wherever you look
beware those who've only read one book.

Because they'll not have read that one either
though they put their nose in it forever.

THE CRACKED SOUL

(after Charles Baudelaire's 'La Cloche Fêlée')

It's bittersweet, on winter nights,
huddled by a coalfire as it splutters and smokes,
to listen to church bells chiming through fog,
awakening distant memories from lost days.

How blessed is the bell of vigorous note
that faithfully tolls its religious cry –
like an old soldier, awake all night in his tent –
still hearty and healthy, in spite of age.

But me, my soul is cracked, and when in boredom
it would fill the cold night air with song,
its voice sounds more like a death-rattle

in the throat of a wounded soldier under
a heap of dead and dying, by a lake of blood,
who at last gives up the will to live.

STRAY THOUGHT

I remember how the Foster brothers
trained their birds in stages:
Gobowen, Craven Arms, Frome,
before off they went to Nantes,
Avranches, St Malo, and Bordeaux.

It helped set their compasses for home
and never failed to fill the brothers'
hearts with wonder, every time they
made it to Llandudno – bright and pert,
as if straight out of the ark.

Then a few hapless ones would go astray,
blown off course by gales in the Channel
or hit by the peregrine. Others
more of my persuasion, settled,
disorientated, high on cathedral rooftops

and, peering down, opted for
the life they saw below, among
baguette crumbs and croissant flakes
under little metal chairs and tables
outside cafés where

lovers sat billing and cooing
and solitary souls on
a caffeine/Gauloise fix

gazed down the cobbled streets
at the spectre of liberty.

THE SLIP

I keep going back to it
and it keeps coming back to me –
a pendulum's to-and-fro,
while the clock spins in slo-mo
marking time like Zeno.
And none of it that long ago.

The poignant photograph,
the love letter, the frisson
of monochrome hardship
on the breadline. Wild-eyed
cannon fodder at the frontline.
Even my own black-and-white youth.

All lost now behind the times.
Though time doesn't exist –
on mantelpiece or wrist
neither zone by zone
nor hourglass grain by grain
nor corncrake's crexing,
over and over again.

Still I give it house-room
and let it beat its little drum
and bear its one-eyed witness
until kingdom come.
While I look to live outside it
in the moment
whenever I can give it the slip.

A SWATHE

Something clings to memory
long after sorrow for the 'dear departed',
the 'sadly missed', subsides
and places look at us over their shoulder,
as they move on. And the notice of death
takes barely a couple of lines.
Any place you come to will
tell you the same story, only
with different fates and names.

Of what I remember, thinned
but growing back with every sweep of the scythe,
what really happened? The day Mrs Farrell
slipped and bled to death
on Laundry Hill? Or the night
Miss Treharne the Classicist
walked into the sea and drowned.
Her private tragedy made public
in the mouth of a morning tide.

Or the summer afternoon
Peter Crossley was killed
cycling on the coast road.
The day David Vaughan passed away,
a wraith among us playing
only a few days before.
How randomly now and who knows why
they spring to mind who left
this life before their time.

THE PARAPET

Some days I wait, distracted at melancholy's front line
where the ghosts come out to haunt what's left of time.

No tragedians among them. The recruit who fell too soon
to show what might become of him, his stare frozen

in a picture frame, and on the back his name, Frank –
who fell at the Somme and stands for all whose star sank

below the parapet like his, that February night.
Or heard the messenger knocking at first light

at a door by the signal box in Oakham.
I knew the ones that got the telegram.

And Uncle Joe who took one in the lung. Not quite fatal.
His doom to instruct conscripts how to fire a rifle.

'Cannon-fodder,' he'd say, 'all soon to die.
Sometimes, you know, it brought tears to the eye.'

To hear him cough you'd wonder how he kept the will to live
on into his eighties, racked for breath. And yet he seemed to thrive.

Black-buttoned bastards they called his regiment.
You could sense in him, even then, just what they meant.

His wit a bayonet, the only way he knew to grieve.
I see them all there now, in No Man's land, as if they're still alive.

My mother's folk, looking across from somewhere in Book Six,
mouthing something I can't quite lipread, about the Styx

and its tributaries, those rivers our *bateaux-ivres* must navigate until
our number's up, and all is done and said, for good or ill.

All that was and is no more, in a lifetime's here-and-now,
with its myriad deaths in tow and myriad births to follow.

ZERO HOURS

And yet they're long
and steal the day
away from under me.
What tomorrow might bring
who can tell?

Turn up with a will
to hear 'Not today…'
Or the call comes in
to drop everything
and write this down.

COCKTAIL HOUR

Earth is sober, not a drop has ever passed its lips.
It is the line the officer asks you to walk.
Grave can be the laws of gravity.

They point the middle way that some prefer
to the fiction that uplifts the soul,
at an unstable zinc table like this one.

The sea for neighbour, raising an elbow
and setting it down, to the chatter
of ice-cubes and melting shingle.

Intoxication of momentary revelation.
Sheer unreality. The poem hallucinating,
waving its claw in the air.

MOBY DICK

I

These days I also set my course
by memory and sound alone.

The gasboiler kicks in and the house
creaks against the pier.

The commuters defrost their cars.
I hear their desperate scraping

trying to get out – running late
before they cast off and are gone

wherever they fish for their pay
in the deep tides beyond my horizon.

II

I spend my time and my pension
netmending my mind as best I can

through hurricane after hurricane
of the world's troubles and my own –

the unseen iceberg down below.
What underwrites the lifeboat now?

No more than the tale I escape to tell
thinking of Melville and Ishmael?

Queequeg and the great White Whale –
evermore never more at peril.

A LEAD WEIGHT

I moved on from lead-piping and brass wire
and the melting pot on the Primus, the sand,
the cigar-tube, the ends of copper pipe,
casting fishing-weights for my paternoster –
to this mess of pottage: words, thoughts,
the fish being now fished out,
and faith alone surviving in my heart. Though
sorely tested on the ground by ruin and
destitution everywhere I cast an eye.

DISPLACED

Then you feel its pulse under your feet,
as a poem should, beating up through you
as the boat meets the open sea.
You might drown now in the thrill
of heartless heartful bow-wave and wake,
as in the closing time of the world
and after-hours behind locked doors.

To wake up in morning-after reverie,
in a swivel chair, facing the window
and staring into a full fathom five-yard
horizon as it soaks this October day

in Atlantic rain like a flock of migrant
sea-birds that have lost their way
and seem somehow to have scattered

across the shire and its ploughings
and harrowings and sowings of the winter
wheat; and the tufted wind soars like
a lapwing of recent memory and calls
like a forgotten curlew, suddenly
pleading for an end to sorrow
and depletion, and the soul's exile.

I sell myself a yarn that says it's like
finding where the fish are to be found.
Somehow it displaces me, as
the local accent I was born to caught
in a crowd of strangers will.
As if it were as true a way to be
as risking all somewhere off Rockall.

A HOLIDAY IN THE YORKSHIRE DALES

Once days knew their place. There were norms,
as hard now to believe as to remember.
According to the lunar motions
expect equinoctial gales and storms
to order, by the calendar. September
teetering, March all lambs and lions.

Now we go by *bateau-ivre* downhill
courtesy of the 'weather event',
out through time's floodgates,
where people with names like Fothergill

('further river') and Arkwright lament
washed-out shows and fetes…
ruined homes, sandbagged streets.

We wave them farewell like Noah
as down we dash to catastrophe
remembering how life once ran slower,
lapped by a green incorruptible sea.
But no longer. Now days are in uproar,
out to get even with you and me.

DECEMBER WITH FIELDFARES

December in a hole and still digging
its resting place for winter wreckage –
its dark age lit by a weak sun
at last at standstill, tools laid down
for home and new year nativity.

A pagan still, chorused by the field-travellers
as they crowd the air – teeth-chatterers,
shiverers, older than Vikings, raiding
South to gorge on haw and sloe,
their breast-bones brushed with snow.

They sweep and settle, a-flutter, and
hurtle away again, with rush of wings,
to scatter, to alight further on
in growing murk. They bring no lesson
but seem a lesson to be learnt.

MARGARET YOU GRIEVE FOR

'Margaret, are you grieving
Over Goldengrove unleaving?'
G.M. Hopkins

When I hear them cry
            'Save the Planet!'
I know they're really
            grieving for Margaret.

O the Planet won't die
            but sigh with relief
to wave goodbye
            to Margaret and her grief.

ON MAKING IT BACK

So we go down, all of us, in time.
Some perished in the lifeboat,
some nowhere to be found,
vessels wrecked and minds
of those who lived to tell the tale:
Gulliver talking to the horses,
Ishmael of the whale and me
listening for the corncrake.

NOW

Somewhere, between coinbox and switchboard,
by undersea cable, and now; between old and
new, I go, struggling as before to come to terms

with change, from the coins that once jingled in my pocket
to the 5G all-singing network of the hour.

I remember when time existed as distance,
when operators were no smarter than the rest of us,
their bakelite headphones more like ear-muffs
muffling submarine sound, putting you through
now, as if now were an aperture to squeeze

the world into, for three minutes, before
you must insert more change, standing there
in the dank phonebox, in the rainswept light
of a November evening. How, hit or miss,
we tried to catch each other in.

Am I thinking of value? Not quantity but quality?
Not triumph but adversity? The hard-won word,
then silence and waiting in-between, knowing
I will see you before you hear from me again,
whenever that will be.

What does waiting mean? Is it nothing anymore?
Once when the postman would pass without stopping,
he'd wave as he went, knowing as he did the meaning
of your hopes or fears. Care, now, all unseen. Now itself,
a blur of ping-pong chats, or a sudden video call.

Time enriched or trivialised? Or life as before
by other means? Though anyone reading here will soon
need commentary to know: what I – whoever I was –
am talking about; how being itself might change.
How hard it is to live without forgetting.

THE MORNING AFTER

But we don't have to be dead to forget
and be forgotten. No matter what,
blitzed brain-cells can only fail when
trying to retrace their steps, between
the night before and the morning after,
especially by such frail light as the dawn
served up on those winter days
of storm's aftermath, and you leant there
with your cup of tea for hair-of-the-dog,
limpet-eyed and barnacled inside
wondering what kind of fool you were
this time. Except the crowd were all
in the same boat and had no idea either
but their own share of misgivings
and alcohol's mood-swings to see them
through the day till opening time.

SKYE BOAT SONG

letter to John and Bar Purser, Alan and Rae Riach

The wide load on the road to Skye
was a boat, neither bonny nor speedy,
a working boat, weathered and fouled,
symbol of struggle in a world
far from leisure, or that old romance
over the water. A no-nonsense
fishing boat that slowed us down
in the torn light of a windblown
February evening. Slowed us
each into our little privacies...

dreaming awake of mysteries,
unknotting tangles in the mind,
hurts and hopes of every kind.

Brexit glooming over Scotland,
the latest cauchemar out of England.
Send it home to think again:
Enlightened Scotland must Remain,
by auld alliance, European…

Still the world's work trailed behind,
taking forever to unwind:
politics that come nowhere close
to what we are and what life is,
both for better and for worse.
Not that it's art's task to mend the curse
or swear allegiance to a cause
but to sober and delight us
beyond the heights of *katharsis*
to dwell among difficulties.

* * *

So as we crept, I thought all this.
I thought of a swan in the streets of Paris.
I thought of an albatross on deck.
I thought of us behind that truck
and how we groaned and cried 'Oh fuck!'
grinding along at ten miles an hour
and no way round to overtake her.
Until the escort led her off the road
to let us pass and gather speed:
over the bridge, a bird on the wing,
heading for Drinan like a song –

now hurtling down a single track
headlights plunging in the dark
until, half-dazed, there we were,
stepping out in wild weather
the croft lurching at its epicentre
in drunken *son-et-lumière*.

And not too late for cocktail hour
with peat-smoke and whisky-sour,
and crabmeat – Purser style. Music
in the air and argument, as quick-
witted as the road had been slow.
While round the croft the black wind blew
from America and down the flue
gusting smoke and Atlantic air
just to remind us where we were.
The talk swirling too with a passion.

Choose delight or resignation:
choose Nietzsche, or Schopenhauer.
(If you ask me, choose neither.)
Choose brother Jack over WB.
Choose! declare your loyalty.
Seek truth in the ordinary.
Don't stretch metaphor too far.
So said one and then another...
Be hard too on your own kind
is truest service to mankind.
Be hard on yourself and the Word
if you'd make a better world.

That's far enough in any weather –
and lay it by in wonder.

Then speaking of an island
as a theatre in the round,
in the spirit of the moment
someone exclaimed:
'Skye's not an Isle but a continent,
the mainland of the Hebrides'.
It struck a chord, in many quays,
from Castle Bay's to Port Righ's.
So whisky-sours worked their spell
until thought ebbed and time stood still.
All turning then to bed and sleep
under a gusting roof; and deep
down, into the natural obscurity
of things, and of life's tragedy, as we
sank to the bottom of the sea.

* * *

The wren was in the wall at the window
wiring up the day. The cloud so low
I saw no world beyond but rain
and mist. All I saw was the wren
in the wall, busily going out and in.
The king of all birds... *plentyn bach*
hwi-hwi dru an bach.
Little child, poor little thing,
where are you going? Where are you going
with your five-note song?
With your tinker's soldering iron:
your up-with-the-kettle, down-with-the-pan
O dreolin? my little electrician.
Risen spirit of St Stephen.
Leitmotif to my heart's aubade.

What poetry of life you've made
with your welder's torch
and running repairs, to birch
and furze, and blowing rowan,
rain- and wind-swept drystone,
never a doubt or singer's block
but ever steady like a rock
where the burn goes clattering down.
Your *ceol mor* enough to drown
the world's lunatic din.
O master of unacknowledged legislation! –
mercurial messenger, in whose eye
shines all there's to see
and know of human vanity.

All living things must die, I fear,
but love and music will endure.

So I heard you in the day's first light
while Croft No. 3 Drinan slept late
soon enough to stir and wake
as the cattle homed like clockwork
dead on the hour of eight
and lined up at the gate
for their licks and fodder.

* * *

Otherwise, a day to leave to the weather,
to keep indoors till things got better.
To talk and read. For Riach and Purser
to put copy together
for *The National* – 'The world's worst newspaper'

according to Gove the Quisling Brexiter,
his *worst* the best endorsement ever.

Now enter Scotland by total
immersion. Choose Occidental.
Choose medieval-metaphysical.
Revive the Celtic Revival.
Our people ever were impractical?
No, they were poor and downtrodden.
Vulnerable to superstition.
Don't ever let that be forgotten
by either poet or musician –
though some were saints for certain
and others visionaries.
Bring the Irish back to the Hebrides?
The only problem, they refuse
to come, or find common cause
in history or language.
Ask them over at the Alamo
of Sabhal Mòr. They'll tell you
but only if you speak their lingo.
Meanwhile make music.
Revel in dram and *craic*.
How Purser walked to see MacLean
all the way by loch and Cuillin –
musician to poet – from Drinan
to Braes, and back again,
in a tale from ancient Japan
a Hebridean *hommage* à la Zen.
Pupil to master beyond the mountain.
As told so well by Paddy Bushe
with eloquence and rare finesse
not on a choppy sea like this
aboard a *bateau* out of water.

* * *

Never was there greater need to stir
to take the air along the shore
where nevermore meets evermore
down through the birchwood glade
where the burn plunges and time's made
to race and halt about itself
and what's not surefooted comes to grief
and nothing's surefooted enough.

Here, below the remains of Dún Liath,
by the ruin of the Laird's grave,
halt a moment and make time
to hear his tenants' chorus:
'Tread down! Tread down on him!
Tread down on him as he trod down on us!'
Still resounding through the wood
as with heart and soul they tread
the sods down in bitter hatred.
Hearts dark with wit and anger.

Hear them and remember
their hard lives led far from leisure,
or romance over the water.
As on Sleat's coast across the way
where Irish myth tells its story
of Cú Chulainn at Dún Scáith
schooled in arms by Skathach,
the shadowy warrior maid.
'Pause in wonder,' as Riach said.
'Then try to find your way back.'
So I've tried and am trying still
but with what meta- to the physical?

And so I wondered… as there we stood
on Slappin's shore below the wood
as sun at last turned grey cloud
to gauze and sent it on its way
thinning as far as we might see
towards the Cuillins' majesty
now as if painted by Paul Henry
over from Connemara on holiday.

* * *

And then another round we made that night
but sleepier and not so late
with music at our cradle: 'Corn Bunting',
'Airy Plover' and MacIntosh lamenting,
'Isobel Mackay', with pipes dispensing
poignant melancholy; ineffable
pibroch from Rideout's fiddle,
'Dreaming of Islands' to escape our trouble –
all at our leisure, in a stolen break…

Now try to find your way back.

Wherever that is to the like of us,
tenants of a half-way mad house.

Still, next morning we must board
and wave farewell, to sail the road.
And as we went, defragged and
ready for the fray, that wide load
came to mind again, and a question:
whether its boat had been bound
for a breaker's yard or the ocean.

Much as I wonder here and now
about the future, and my letter to you.

CASTAWAY

I knew all along there'd come a day
that would turn out to be today,
and I must say goodbye to the island,
and so to my life: a castaway in
spirit and letter, adrift on
England's darkling plain.

Certain that where, and whatever, days
came down to, and however I got by,
there'd be no going back to then –
when life was lived in the round –
and I drained my glass to the last,
staring into the middle-distance

meditating, making up my mind,
as I've tried ever since to do here:
making to stay something, as an island does,
coming and going on the horizon,
holding its ground in the tide
through the vagaries of weather.

A SONG

Snow chalked to windward through the little wood,
monochrome, as if on scraper-board.
Look closely and find traces of new life on pause
in the thin cold. Human-seeming, heart-ruled,

up-lifting as a lapwing cloud's inside-outwardness,
fugitive from harder weather, from winter
in the ground that keeps us dormant,
towards light that wakes us, leaking from
the curtain, earlier and earlier, a sign
to follow like a star to a miracle –
crocus at the door, green washed through
everything, that will hold its ground and grow,
and somewhere birds already nesting
without letting on anything is happening
(god's honour) betrayed only by a song.

OPENING-TIME

What is it to open time?
The bolt drawn, the door
unlocked and the barman
poised to pour

your poison of choice
into the bottomless glass
of the mirror behind him
and the mirrors in the mirror

where you see yourself
receding, farther and farther
through the course of the evening
until at last time closes.

A NIGHT ON THE HEATH

What stalked through the Post Office?

The weather's foul again, ripping through
the unnameable archipelago.
And here am I, fumbling with truth,
longing to unbutton, like Vladimir Holan,
that time he drank Hamlet under the table,
while history went falsely drawn past his window
like the Vlatava river in flood.

Who am I? Wandering the night,
buttonholing ghosts, demanding to know
what is the State without love?
Living death. Cases alter circumstances.
But power's no ghost, as Hamlet learnt,
struggling between past and present,
old and new, the lot of all poets.

How losers outnumber victors –
just as the dead form the majority. Tell me
what that might mean for democracy?
A promotion for historians?
A lifeline for gravediggers.
It's not so much who comes out on top as how.

When at last I found him he said,
'Whenever they tell me it's all about family,
I laugh. Life's not short enough
for that to hold its ground.
Ask Hamlet and he came nowhere close
at about the age of Christ.'

The kingdoms would tear themselves apart
but lack the votes or muscle.
The powers pump up the volume on God Save the Queen.
Fortinbras grinds his teeth.
I wait for the sorting office
to redirect me to the republic.

ASK

Ask a fish what the ocean's like
and it'll go where you don't dare.

Ask a bird what the sky is like
and it'll take off through the air.

Ask me what life is like
and I'll show you the door.